PRAISE FOR

Tell It Like It Is

This is practical theology at its best. The book is theologically grounded, reflects on actual practice, and provides a useful model for all our churches. We learn that the gift of testimony not only strengthens worship and community caring, testimony can even reshape administration and committee meetings. The book is itself the testimony of a gifted and wise pastor, and like all faithful testimony, it convicts us and changes us, too.

> David Bartlett, Professor of New Testament,
> Columbia Theological Seminary

In this beautifully written book, Lillian Daniel describes the practice of testimony: people standing up in community worship and telling stories about how they have experienced God. A simple definition perhaps, but Daniel movingly and thoughtfully shows how complex, powerful, risky, and life changing testimony can be. Here, people speak with wonder, joy, and astonishment about the places where the pathways of their lives have intersected the trajectories of God's presence and grace. With candor, theological insight, and pastoral wisdom, Daniel describes how testimony can deeply affect, and finally transform, the life of a congregation. Prepare to learn here about the practice of testimony, but prepare also to be touched by the courage and honesty of people speaking aloud their experiences of faith.

> Thomas G. Long, Bandy Professor of Preaching,
> Candler School of Theology, Emory University

Already an enormously gifted writer, preacher, and pastor, Lillian Daniel has done in this book something quite audacious—and wonderfully welcome. She's had the good sense to think about the church with the aid of the people who actually live it and make it. This wisdom comes as a book about how recovering a homegrown practice of testimony helped transform one congregation. But in her hands the story becomes an enticing and full ecclesiology rooted in experience and empowered by hope. She hears and speaks the church into being here, and it's a joyous discovery. Testify away!

> Wes Avram, Clement-Muehl Assistant Professor of
> Communication, Yale Divinity School

Great worship is alive and a bit unpredictable. It wakes us up. And drawing us to the edge of our seat, it draws us over the edge of how we've always thought about things, how we've always thought about the people sitting next to us. Daniel's book tells the story of one congregation who learned that the power to make their gatherings alive and transformative lay not in a program or in technology, but in themselves—their own simple and profound stories of how they met God in various disguises and the difference it made. Oh, that more pastors and congregations could learn the same!

> Mary Sellon, coauthor of *Practicing Right Relationship* and *Redeveloping the Congregation*

This marvelous book by Lillian Daniel is so much more than a book *about* testimony. The book itself is a testimony to the powerful ways God works when people are invited to tell others what they have seen and heard and touched of God's presence in their lives. These pages are populated with real people who may have more questions than answers. And yet, by speaking from the heart, they point us to the mysterious reality that crackles just below the surface of life. Without question, this book has the power to transform congregations, as Daniel's own congregation was wondrously transformed by the practice of testimony.

> Martin B. Copenhaver,
> Wellesley Congregational Church

While many church members sing "I Love to Tell the Story," the sad truth is that too few do. Many either don't tell the story or, when they do tell it, feel anxious or fretful, making it a far from loving experience. Lillian Daniel's book offers wise advice about engaging a congregation in the practice of testimony—sharing stories of faith that enliven both the hearers and sharers. She offers us a new look at an old tradition that many mainline congregations have abandoned. And in doing so she shows how testimony, bearing witness, breathes new life into people and the congregations they love.

> J. Brent Bill, author of *Holy Silence: The Gift of Quaker Spirituality*

Tell It Like It Is

Tell It Like It Is

RECLAIMING THE PRACTICE OF TESTIMONY

LILLIAN DANIEL

THE
ALBAN
INSTITUTE

Herndon, Virginia
www.alban.org

The Alban Institute
2121 Cooperative Way, Suite 100
Herndon, VA 20171-3025

Unless otherwise noted, Scripture quotations in the preface are from the Holy Bible, New International Version, copyright © 1973, 1978, 1984, International Bible Society, and are used by permission of Zondervan Publishing House.

Scripture quotations in chapter 7 and that marked (NRSV) in the preface are based on the New Revised Standard Version of the Bible, copyright © 1989, Division of Christian Education of the National Council of Churches of Christ in the United States of America, and are used by permission.

Cover design by R+B Design Firm.

Library of Congress Cataloging-in-Publication Data

Daniel, Lillian.
    Tell it like it is : reclaiming the practice of testimony / Lillian Daniel.
       p. cm.
    Includes bibliographical references.
    ISBN-13: 978-1-56699-318-0
    ISBN-10: 1-56699-318-0
    1. Witness bearing (Christianity)   2. Evangelicalism.   I. Title.
    BV4520.D36 2006
    248'.5—dc22
                                                              2005030948

          10   09   08   07   06   UG   1   2   3   4   5

To The Church of the Redeemer,
United Church of Christ,
New Haven, Connecticut,
on the corner of Whitney Avenue and Cold Spring Street

CONTENTS

In the past few years, I have worshiped at Church of the Redeemer in New Haven several times. On the outside, Redeemer looks the part of staid, New England Congregationalism. Sitting in the shadow of Yale Divinity School, the colonial-style brick building with its soaring white steeple almost defines proper and refined Christianity. As I learned, however, the exterior is deceptive. Redeemer's people are a surprisingly vivacious group. They like to talk. They talk about religious things such as the Bible, social justice, and theology. They talk about church things such as "silver teas," birthdays, deacon elections, the capital campaign, and the Sunday school. They talk about controversial things such as politics, environmentalism, the arts, and poverty. After church, they hang around the coffee hour—for a long time—to talk with their friends. Indeed, these are extroverted Congregationalists.

As I listened, however, I discovered that they were not just chatting. Rather, they talked about things in holy ways, not self-righteously, uncomfortably, or awkwardly. In natural and unaffected ways, they had learned to observe holiness in everyday life, to see God's grace in the world, and they testified to the Spirit's often subtle, and occasionally miraculous, workings in common experience. They had learned to talk about their faith. Redeemer's people testify in formal settings, such as the Sunday service, and informal ones—coffee hour, conversations, Bible studies, and book groups. And they do more than talk. As a community of testifiers, they tell stories in a way that weaves narratives across the congregation. During each visit, I experienced the power of such testimony—the profound honesty of authentic community, a rare awareness of God's presence in the mundane, and a palpable sense of hope. When they first welcomed me, they asked about my story, and I knew they were inviting me into theirs.

All congregations, and all churchgoers, have faith stories. But for much of the twentieth century, mainline Protestants believed that it was somehow impolite or rude to talk about religion. Faith was deeply privatized, an internal matter between the baptized and God. Devotional practices were also private. Indeed, people thought that to talk about faith somehow cheapened it. In that era, Protestants were taught that it was better to walk than talk, taking James's injunction that "faith without works is dead" far more seriously than most Christians throughout history. Social justice, charity, caring for the poor, organizing soup kitchens—mainline Protestants did good works to demonstrate their devotion. Reverence for God meant silence *and* service. Churchgoers, like those at Redeemer, experienced the power of faith in the world through that service. But for many, there was no faith vocabulary, no way of talking about the God whom they served. With no words, it became surprisingly easy to forget the stories. Perhaps this is why both the ancient Hebrews and early Christians wrote down their experiences of God. Without the words, faith would be lost, the service rendered secular. By the end of the twentieth century, mainline Protestantism appeared, to many observers, as faith-*less*—a silent religion with no story to tell. Would a contemporary James change his mind? For the last few decades, mainline Protestantism seems to prove the case: faith without words is dead.

It is in this context that the people of Redeemer learned to speak. For years, they had done good works. Guided by the Holy Spirit and the energetic leadership of their pastor, Lillian Daniel, they learned to talk their walk. In these pages, you will meet the people who make up Redeemer and hear their voices—halting, doubtful, joyful, sad, hopeful, needy, exuberant, and thankful. You will hear them gain confidence in both their own words and God's word. And you will hear Lillian's voice as well tracing through the same steps of growing maturity, and increasing confidence, that God is, indeed, in the midst of an ordinary congregation that chooses to take an extraordinary journey into the grace of storytelling.

Redeemer is not a "perfect" church, and neither is its minister or its people. Indeed, Redeemer's tale of testimony illustrates the beautiful truth that there exists a grace-filled spirituality of imperfection in storytelling communities. The recovery of story makes us more human, more open to our truest selves in God. By intentionally embarking on this risk-filled pilgrimage of testimony, the people of Redeemer unintentionally revitalized their congregation. Once on the verge of closing, Redeemer is again the lively church of its history. Lillian and the members did not start out to fix the church. Their journey began because they wanted to grow in faith. Congregational renewal was a byproduct of learning to take the faith more seriously, as Lillian puts it, "to discover a new word and new life in an old book." As you read their story, you will see that they found both. Engaging the practice of testimony transformed the people, a minister, ministry, and the future of their congregation.

Lillian and the members of Redeemer did not intend to become an instructive example of renewal for mainline Protestant congregations. But they have. Through imagining a new way of words, they found a new way of life together, a way that offers hope to those of us seeking authentic and transformative Christian community. Here is a path, one congregation's pilgrimage to a new place of holy vibrancy and vital faith. Read, enter into their journey, cry, laugh, and rejoice with them, and learn from their wisdom. Let them cast a new vision of church for you and your congregation. Welcome to their story.

Diana Butler Bass
Alexandria, Virginia

PREFACE

I remember having coffee and eggs with a colleague in the ministry, a charismatic and evangelical church pastor. As we sat in the booth of the diner on a busy New Haven street, I was telling her about my new idea for the congregation. "We are introducing the practice of testimony into our church," I proudly explained.

"Why on earth do you want to do that?" she asked, putting down her coffee with an emphatic thud. "If there was one thing I wish I could get rid of in my service, it would be those testimonies!" I had been hoping to gain insights into the testimony tradition from a charismatic pastor who was familiar with it, but I had not expected such a negative reaction.

And so she explained. In her spirit-filled church, the service began with lengthy spontaneous sharing of testimonies offered by whoever felt moved. "You know how it is," she said. "It's the same people getting up every time, using it as a chance to be in the spotlight, taking things over."

In my New England congregation, I could no more imagine my members doing this than I could imagine them suddenly demanding to juggle.

"It's the opposite issue in our church," I explained. "We have to talk people into doing it. They're very shy about talking about their faith."

"I can't imagine," she said, shaking her head in disbelief. And I could not imagine what she was describing either.

While in other free-church services I had witnessed church members simply taking up the microphone and launching into ecstatic praise, claiming Jesus as Lord and Savior, and being caught up in tongues of the Holy Spirit, I knew such expression would not be comfortable for our church. But I also knew that we had a faith story to tell one another. Why couldn't we practice testimony too? Besides, the practice flowed naturally out of our own congregational history, in which new members gave a seven-part conversion narrative before the whole congregation; or the days of the First and Second Great Awakenings, when laypeople were freed to proclaim their own experience of God. Furthermore, given the wide variety of scriptural references to testimony, I knew that what we were doing would be in there somewhere. But my colleague's words chilled me. Was I opening up a Pandora's box I would later want to close? Or would this turn out to be a grand adventure into an old practice that would give us new life?

So often in our congregations, beautiful stories of God float through the church unspoken. This book is the story of one community of faith's journey to learn to give one another's faith stories a hearing. In a world of twisted stories, artifice, and polemics, one New England church wanted to learn to tell a better story about a loving God who lives and breathes in the ordinary spaces of life and, of course, in the local church. We wanted to tell it like it is.

In our mainline Protestant church we defined testimony very simply: it was to be offered as a spoken word in the context of worship, and it could not omit God. That may sound like a ludicrous caveat for the church, for a community of believers, but it is my experience as a pastor that many church members have great difficulty expressing their faith. We had lost the art and practice of testimony.

Rediscovering Testimony in Scripture

To rediscover the practice, I first turned to Scripture, beginning with the most obvious form of recorded testimony, the book of Psalms. When read or sung in worship, psalms are not considered testimony, for in that case, we are not speaking out of our own original experience. But we are recalling someone's testimony from the past that so spoke to the shared community's experience of God that it became codified and ritualized. When we do recite the psalms, we recall another's testimony and make it our own. We uplift one another, or testify to the pain of human existence, but always in the light of God. The psalms may be sad or elated, but God is always present in them.

The Gospels take us closer to the definition of testimony that most of us hold, a sense of testimony as words from one believer to the world, expressing the power and presence of God. Perhaps the most familiar scriptures on testimony are found in the Gospel of John. Describing John the Baptist in John 1:7, the apostle wrote: "He came as a witness to *testify* concerning that light, so that through him all men might believe." A testifier is not the light, but points us toward the light of God.

John 3:11 reminds us that testimony is not always well received, even when it is ultimately good news: "I tell you the truth, we speak of what we know, and we *testify* to what we have seen, but still you people do not accept our testimony." In John 7:7, Jesus says, "The world cannot hate you, but it hates me because I *testify* that what it does is evil." In James 5:3 we can feel the sting of these words: "Your gold and silver are corroded. Their corrosion will *testify* against you and eat your flesh like fire. You have hoarded wealth in the last days." Testimony, our congregation learned, is risky and unpopular at times, for it may have within it a critique of the world around us.

The book of Acts is another rich source for testimony, in which the early Christians go about the work of testifying and witnessing in earnest. In Acts 4:33, testimony is associated with great spiritual power: "With great power the apostles continued to *testify* to the resurrection of the Lord Jesus, and much grace was upon them all." Testimony, we gather from Acts, grew the church and helped to accomplish Christ's mission after the resurrection. Our church came to understand this, as we saw that our testimonies started to transform us as a community. In Acts the change immediately following that testimony was pretty dramatic: "There was not a needy person among them, for as many as owned lands or houses sold them and brought the proceeds of what was sold. They laid it at the apostles' feet, and it was distributed to each as any had need." (NRSV) That must have been some testimony. But even in our church, we would discover that testimony has a rhetorical function. It produces not just believers, but doers of the word. Testimony can be a call to action and to a more passionate relationship with God.

Paul, as one whose entire life is given purpose in his testimony, exemplifies this passion the most in Acts 20:24: "However, I consider my life worth nothing to me, if only I may finish the race and complete the task the Lord Jesus has given me—the task of *testifying* to the gospel of God's grace." Similarly in Acts 26:5, testimony includes confession, so that the hearer might appreciate the distance traveled: "They have known me for a long time and can *testify*, if they are willing, that according to the strictest sect of our religion, I lived as a Pharisee." Many of our testimonies would turn out to be confessional, and provocatively so.

In Paul's own words from his many letters, we see a wider definition in which testimony is not just about God and the individual speaker, but about the community of believers as well. In my own church the testimonies often spoke about how God worked through the church, and they sound much like Paul's words from so long ago in 2 Corinthians 8:3: "For I *testify* that they gave as much as they were able, and even beyond their ability," or in somewhat less flattering words from Romans 10:2: "For I can *testify* about them that they are zealous for God, but their zeal is not based on knowledge." Paul testifies to the state of the community in its relationship to God, and while sometimes it is good news, there is correction as well, as in Galatians 4:15, when he looks back at a better time in the community and says: "What has happened to all your joy? I can *testify* that, if you could have done so, you would have torn out your eyes and given them to me." And he goes on to worry in Galatians 4:16, "Have I now become your enemy by telling you the truth?" Again, testimony has its risks.

The scriptural references to testimony are varied but consistent on a few points. People of faith are called to testify to God's power and presence in their lives, and in the New Testament this is a call to proclaim Christ. Testimony, according to Scripture, will not be easy or necessarily well received, but we are called to do it anyway. And lastly, testimony seems to be most dramatic when it takes place in community, and serves to build up the faith. Here, as a pastor, I respond most to Paul's letters, and the manner in which he moved with agility between testimony about God to testimony about God in the small communities of faith he loved, just as we would turn out to move in our local church.

Testimonies from the Past Led Us into the Future

As it turned out, when we as a church gave our testimonies, there was less about Jesus than there was about God. There was also less about God than there was about the local church. But for a congregation within the denomination the United Church of Christ, we are not theologically bound to convert one another to a saving faith in Jesus, per se, in order to save nonbelievers from damnation. In fact, this notion would seem absurd to most of our members, who feel an opposite call to respect people of other faiths and their beliefs. So it makes sense denominationally that when we did testify, our words were often about the gathered community, and about one another. God was not absent, but God was revealed in a very grass roots Congregational way, in which the divine was present in the ordinariness of community life.

To understand this, and to search for roots, I turned to a few examples of testimonies from New England's history. With a rancorous tone, Increase Mather (1639–1723) gave his 1687 testimony, not for something, but against something as well, in his remarks entitled "Testimony against prophane customs: namely, health drinking, dicing, cards, Christmas-keeping, New Year's gifts, cock-scaling, saints' days, etc." Clearly, testimony has been used as a shaper of communities, to differentiate one church's practices from another's, as we see here in Mather's attempt to convince Congregationalists to forswear both secular gaming and the religious practices of the Church of England, all under the rubric of offering his testimony. Testimonies have always been more than an opportunity to express oneself in light of God's grace. Testimonies have also had a rhetorical function, the ability to shape and mold the community of listeners.

Dealing with a more serious issue than card playing, in 1733 Elihu Coleman gave and then had printed his testimony "against that antichristian practice of making slaves of men: wherein it is shewed to be contrary to the dispensation of the law and time of the Gospel, and very opposite both to grace and nature." The fact that these testimonies were offered with the goal of convincing believers to behave a certain way, here to abolish slavery, and then published to extend their persuasive function is of great interest to me. For even at Church of the Redeemer in the twenty-first century, more than three hundred years later, I discovered that we Congregationalists would still offer our testimonies to persuade and reform the church and the world.

Despite the historical recordings of testimony, for the most part, testimony does not thrive as a practice in my denomination anymore. Today it is more a practice of the free church tradition, or evangelicalism. Yet by looking back at past testimonies, I could see the same yearnings and longings that remain. So by borrowing this practice of testimony from other churches that use testimony today, I was really returning to a tradition that my own denomination had once treasured but since lost.

Yet testimony is not traditionally a practice that we associate with justice-seeking churches. Testimony has become a practice that makes us think of one individual speaking about a relationship with a personal savior. But in rediscovering this practice in a mainline church, and recovering its history, I saw that we bring our ecclesiology to the practice. So one of the concerns I had when we, a liberal Protestant congregation, began the practice of testimony was that these moments would become soapbox speeches. I worried that people who felt strongly about politics, for instance, might use the opportunity to speak about their pet political issue, and alienate others. Yet, to say that testimony must be devoid of anything political or controversial is not true to the practice, or to understanding that God is involved in all aspects of our lives, with a porous boundary between the church and the public square. After all, we were the descendants of the Puritans whose church was also the town's meetinghouse. We made the practice our own, as other congregations can as well. Testimony has so much richness that it should not be embraced by only one style of Christian, just as no segment of the church should cast it aside. We can all bring to testimony the rich variety of Christ's church, as well as the wideness of God's mercy. All Christians, even reserved protestant New Englanders, can grow in their faith when they learn to talk to one another about God, and really tell it like it is.

Many testimonies from my own Congregationalist history are against one thing or another. Many rail in favor of one theological position or another. But many are full of the very same longing, faith, and mystery that I experience in the twenty-first century. And sometimes a testimony was recorded in history that sounds so much like one from a Congregational church today, that I am stunned. Even while I cannot imagine what exactly it was like to be there, in that different time, I find myself aware of the Holy Spirit's presence when I read words like these from Anne Wilcox, from Stockbridge, Massachusetts, in the 1830s:

I shall now attempt to describe my feelings. They was first wrought upon, when I was absent from this place. I think the first cause derived, from my hearing of the revival in Stockbridge. I soon felt dejected, & unworthy to be here in such an interesting time. But still I was anxious to return, & to come home with a strong determination to obtain an interest in the Saviour if possible. I felt as if then was the <accepted> time, if ever. & I trust it was. The first meeting I attended after my return here, was with a heavy heart, & ready to break with anguish under a sense of my situation. The Lord saw fit to strive with me, 2 or 3 weeks, before he made me willing to submit wholly to his will. In that time, I attempted often to Pray, but when I returned to my room it was with a heart as heavy as when entered. I was anxious to read the Bible, & found many very precious promises for those that would seek the Lord diligently, which encouraged me still to go on, but I found that I was entirely dependent & that I must throw myself upon the hands of a just & offended God & that I could do nothing but to plead guilty abandoned [illegible deletion] creature. I think I can say from that time I obtained much relief in my mind, & much comfort in Prayer, & in reading the Bible, I found it to be quite a new book to me. & my sincere Prayer is that I may ever continue in the same, & may it be of others for me.[1]

From almost two hundred years ago, I can hear in this woman's testimony a similar message to those that I have heard over the last years in my church—a story of a person lost, dejected, and then, by God's grace, finding meaning. Her opening words have a modern feel: "I shall now attempt to describe *my feelings.*" So much of the power of testimony comes from the risk the speaker takes to describe feelings, all kinds of feelings, not just the happy feelings that society praises us for but the feelings of loss, misery, and confusion as well.

Not all our testimonies at church in New Haven were emotional, but most were. People who in normal conversation might be described as reserved or even aloof revealed a depth of feeling in their testimonies that took us by surprise. It was not so much a display of emotion, or dramatic presentation or reading, but more the depth of emotion in the words chosen. Much like Anne Wilcox's statement, "I shall now *attempt* to *describe* my feelings," it was clear that while this was not coming naturally or easily, something precious was about to be revealed. Testimony involves the risk of sharing feelings, not just any feelings, but those feelings related to the experience of God, or the lack of that experience as well.

Wilcox does not offer a dry theological analysis of her experience but rather a theology rooted in experience. She draws in her context, here a revival in Stockbridge that returned her home confused, longing and yet uplifted, ready to search further for God. And for her now, the Bible has become "a new book."

I recall one modern testimony in our church offered by Sue, a new member, who said:

> As I got older, I felt lonely, as if I had no tether, no sense of a home port. Yet I knew that I didn't need to belong to an institution. Later I attended several churches in different locations that I lived. But it was much easier not to make a commitment. Soccer games, yard work, catching up on errands, etc. But I knew God knew that I believed.
>
> Then the big void occurred in my life. The black hole swallowed me up and got the better part of me. But I think that God knew I believed. I think!

Sue went on to describe how she tentatively began attending Redeemer, with her fiancé and his mother, and she continued: "I came several times and found myself actually reading the bulletin to see what the sermon was about. I even heard the sermon and pondered on the message. Holy Smoke! What a change!"

For Sue in the present, as for Anne Wilcox in the 1830s, the Bible was becoming a new book. As one who has rediscovered testimony, I am struck by the tone of the two testimonies, even as the language and idioms were so different. As people of the Word, throughout Christian history, we have helped one another to discover a new word and new life in an old book. We are always teaching each other how to tell it like it is.

ACKNOWLEDGMENTS

I thank the Lilly Endowment and the Louisville Institute for many opportunities to develop my pastoral imagination. But in particular, I am grateful to have been a part of the first Pastor's Working Group under the leadership of Craig Dykstra and David Wood, and for that group's encouragement in my writing. This project began there. It continued to blossom in the Hartford Seminary Doctor of Ministry program, and I am grateful to my program advisor, Jane Smith, and my teachers Nancy Ammerman and Kelton Cobb. I also thank the Writers Asylum at the St. John's Ecumenical Institute in Collegeville, Minnesota, where this book was finished.

I am grateful to God for many holy friendships that encouraged this work: Wes Avram, Tracey Bergman, Rodney Clapp, Verlee Copeland, Amy Laura Hall, Verity Jones, Rich Kirchherr, Shawnthea Monroe, Deanna Thompson, Susan Townsley, and Cynthia Terry; for my Vermont writing group:

Martin Copenhaver, Dale Rosenberger, and David Wood; for my two editors over the years at *The Christian Century* magazine, Don Ottenhoff and Richard Kaufman; as well as my editor at the Alban Institute, Beth Gaede.

I am grateful to my children, nine-year-old Abigail and twelve-year-old Calvin, who inspire me with the testimony of their large spirits.

To my father, Leon, the writer, and to my mother, Carobel, the storyteller.

To my husband, Lou, whose work and life testify to God's love.

And finally, thanks to the members of the Church of the Redeemer, New Haven, Connecticut, whose testimonies have taught me so much, and to the members of the First Congregational Church, Glen Ellyn, Illinois, who teach me now.

May we all continue to tell God's story in our own words.

INTRODUCTION

Tell It Like It Is

As the 2000 Lenten season ran its course at a traditional looking mainline Protestant church in New Haven, behind the clear glass windows, in the middle of our worship service, something unusual was happening. We had been hearing testimonies. People were standing up at the lectern during worship, sharing with one another the stories of their faith. We were engaged in the ancient Christian practice of testimony.

Of course we had too many attorneys in the congregation to call them "testimonies." For that matter, we had too many people on the run from traditions that do call them "testimonies." So at the Church of the Redeemer we called these statements made by laypeople during worship "Lenten reflections." But they fell in the category of the Christian practice of testimony.

About a year before, our church book group devoured *Practicing Our Faith*, edited by Dorothy Bass. We discussed one practice each session, and the conversation was lively. Everybody wanted to hear more about discernment, and saying yes and saying no. These were spiritual practices that could help group members deal with the busiest of lives. The chapter on Sabbath keeping was more challenging. Could this group keep Sabbath and at the same time lead a frenetically active

Congregational church where we are always one step away from works righteousness?

The chapter that drew the least conversation was the one by Thomas Hoyt Jr. on testimony. Hoyt, a New Testament scholar, was also writing as a bishop on the Christian Methodist Episcopal Church, a denomination in which testimony was more common than it was for us as Congregationalists. So when we read his description of how he was nurtured as a boy in the practice of testimony, members of our book group told stories of churches where they had heard testimonies. But clearly these churches were, to them, like New York City— nice places to visit but not places you would want to live.

But Hoyt's chapter was not limited to just one Christian tradition. Where he laid out a vision of testimony beyond words, our group came on board, immediately understanding how serving a meal at a shelter was a form of testimony. But our group read the descriptions of people speaking out loud in worship about their faith as if they were reading an anthropology article, an intriguing description of what other people from some entirely different culture did.

Hoyt described testimony this way:

> The testimony of ordinary persons in Sunday morning worship and weeknight prayer meetings is characteristic of worship in the "free church" tradition, where services are relatively informal and expressive. One classic praise testimony, popular in the contemporary Black Church goes like this: "Thank you, God, for waking me up this morning; for putting shoes on my feet, clothes on my back, and food on my table. Thank you, God, for health and strength and the activities of my limbs. Thank you that I awoke this morning clothed in my right mind. . . ." In testimony, a believer de-

scribes what God has done in her life, in words both biblical and personal, and the hands of her friends clap in affirmation. Her individual speech thus becomes part of an affirmation that is shared.[1]

"Why not our church?" I thought to myself as I listened to the group's discussion. "Why couldn't we be testifiers as well? Were we really so different from the people Hoyt described? Or could our faith be expressed like this as well?"

As a minister in a congregation of creative and thoughtful people, I have long worried that we ask for their gifts in all areas of church life except worship. Certainly the singers and the readers have their liturgical place, and the ministry is rich for those who participate. But what about the rest, who might have gifts to share and stories to tell that defy the church staff's ability to script or orchestrate? Could we all share our affirmation of the presence of God with one another?

Looking Back

The Church of the Redeemer was founded in the mid-nineteenth century and originally worshiped in a storefront on Chapel Street, which was the business center of New Haven and close to Center Church on the Green and United Church on the Green, the two churches members had left to form this congregation. One might assume that the Church of the Redeemer originally chose not to invest their resources in a grand building, having split away from two of the grandest in New England, but in fact they were already saving up for a grand building of their own.

By 1872 they had built an ornate Victorian affair in the same neighborhood, a building that drew criticism from other

Congregationalists at the time. As a breakaway church, Redeemer's Episcopal-looking building and Lutheran-sounding name reflected a youthful desire to rebel against their dour Congregational parents on the Green.

Today, that 1872 sanctuary, with its multicolored turrets and stained-glass windows, looks like an ornate doll's house of a church. Now shadowed by tall corporate buildings all around, that church building is owned by a small conservative Lutheran congregation struggling with a lack of residents and parking in New Haven's business center.

With a certain savvy, the old Redeemer congregation had seen that the neighborhood around it was changing, and in 1921 they purchased land further north in the East Rock neighborhood that would become home to Yale Divinity School. Congregationalists in a city that their spiritual ancestors, the Puritan settlers, had called "the city on the hill," Redeemer's new plot of land would sit toward the top of that hill, a few blocks below the Georgian cloisters of Yale Divinity School.

Upon purchasing the land, they built themselves an enormous building complex called the "parish house" that they saw as a total Christian life center, complete with a gymnasium, a full kitchen, and an auditorium in which they planned to worship while they built a sanctuary.

Around the time Redeemer was building, surrounding Yale University was capitalizing on Depression-era wages and had completed its greatest building program ever, creating most of the old-fashioned-looking buildings and colleges that today we associate with the university, as well as saving the city by employing the unemployed. The church was not as well off as the university, however, so from the purchase of the land until the laying of the cornerstone of the new sanctuary in 1951, the congregation spent three decades waiting to worship in the church they had dreamed of.

For some years after that, the church was full and thriving, but the decades from the sixties to the nineties were
marked by a rapid decline in membership. As demographics
changed in the 1950s through the 1970s, Redeemer's physical plant continued to reflect the congregation's fortunes. By
the 1970s, after a loss of members to churches in the suburbs
(a common pattern for city churches of the day), the church
made its first backwards move expressed in the physical plant.
The great hall of the parish house in which they once worshiped, the large kitchen, the gymnasium, and some classrooms
were demolished.

The decision had caused great debate and the decision to
demolish had been a close one, resulting in a split in the congregation and more membership loss. The minister was on
the side of demolition, influenced by the fuel crisis of the 1970s
and the cost of heating such a building, and the fact that the
maintenance required to keep it safe was out of the congregation's financial reach. The decision was not made lightly
but was seen as the only way to keep the church solvent. At
this time, a smaller Sunday school area was renovated in an
open-classroom model, and the common areas of the church
were made more inviting and attractive.

In hindsight, we see that the land left vacant after the demolition could have been filled in and used for parking, for at
that time the church owned the house next door. Instead a
grassy pit was left for the nonchurch day care to use as a play-
ground. The next decades were marked by more loss of property, as the church sold the house next door to the church and
the parsonage. The hard decisions to demolish a building or
sell a piece of property were made out of a sense of fiscal
responsibility so that resources would not be squandered but
saved for future generations. The money was put into the endowment to boost the income of a church with a shrinking

pledge base. In the history of the church, you can see a steady progression of entrepreneurial building followed by reversals that seemed to begin just a short time after the grand sanctuary was built, reflecting hope for the future, and then, later, concerns about survival.

Despite the loss of members, the congregation remained vital and was known in the city for the many contributions members made in civic life. The church remained a place of hospitality to many community, theater, and musical groups, and it continued to be a church that fostered the arts community. At one point after the demolition, a positive capital campaign resulted in building a wheelchair ramp into the sanctuary for an aging congregation.

I reflect on the buildings of our church because they tell a story that is not uncommon for mainline churches in urban areas. It is a story of decreasing membership, the decline of resources, a changing city population, and some dispute with the pastors. By the time I arrived at the church, in 1996, the last two ministries had ended in conflict, with members leaving an already shrinking church. After I arrived, I was told that were it not for the money in the endowment, which had grown with the sale of those various church properties and a booming stock market, the church would have, and perhaps should have, closed its doors years before. I was the fourteenth senior minister called to the church, and I wondered in my first days at the church, as the two ministers before me must have wondered, if I might be the last.

But after a year at the church, during which time we began to experience signs of renewal and vitality, I came to realize that what was happening in our congregation was not unique. Despite the statistics on steadily shrinking urban mainline churches, there were also signs of hope in other churches like ours. That first year we received 12 new members, the next year, 25, and we welcomed about that number each year ever since. When I began to serve Church of the Redeemer, we had around 35 people in worship, and the choir might outnumber the congregation. Seven years later we had a worship attendance of about 130, even in our highly transient university community. And perhaps most importantly, the church now includes some previously missing populations—young children, teens, and young singles. As of 2004, the church was recognized nationally as a notable congregation by the Fund for Theological Education for the numbers of future ministers we produced, and by a Lilly Endowment funded project out of Virginia Theological Seminary that recognizes vital mainline congregations rooted in the practices of the faith.

It was in 1999—the beginning of this time of growth in our church, three years into my ministry at Redeemer, and two years after I began course work in the doctor of ministry program at Hartford Seminary—when I began to first consider the possibilities of testimony for our congregation. One phenomenon in particular attracted my attention. We were growing, but pockets of resistance to that growth were beginning to develop. "We're just the right size now," someone might say. "I want to be able to know everyone I go to church with."

How could we grow and maintain our sense of community? How could we tap into the rich resources and talents of our church, and allow the members to give expression to their faith and what it was that was drawing them to Church of the Redeemer? I began to consider whether testimony could be a helpful practice to us in this endeavor, and a doctor of ministry project began to take shape, which later became this book on how we began using testimony, how that practice shaped us as a congregation, and how it continues to sustain the ministry years later.

A Hunger to Express One's Faith

Back in 1999, when I shared the book *Practicing Our Faith* with the book group, I wondered which of these practices might bring us deeper into the faith while lessening the resistance to growth that small churches can feel. Could we share our faith and preserve our intimacy? Despite the book group's lukewarm reaction to the practice of testimony, I believed there was not only a need but a hunger for this sort of opportunity. For one thing, I noticed that our church announcements were getting long again.

Redeemer has a time at the beginning of worship when anyone may come forward to make an announcement. We have a love-hate relationship with this announcement time. On the one hand, it is a chance to see the diverse vitality of the congregation, a chance to match a face and a name to a special event. It is a wonderful introduction for newcomers to the strong lay leadership of our church.

On the other hand, announcements can become long and tedious and interrupt worship. Some announcements overwhelm the listener with details they will never remember, or speak to events that only one or two people might be interested in.

Yet apart from this ongoing struggle with the announcements, I noticed something else was happening. People who could have told you in 30 seconds where and when the community organizing meeting was going to be held were getting up and sharing anecdotes first. People were using the announcements to tell stories, to tell one another in short and perhaps flip ways about themselves and about their faith.

In telling the church about the next community-organizing event, they might testify to the power of the last one and the beauty of seeing all those people of faith together. In telling the church about an adult education opportunity, they might speak first about how it was adult education that drew them into deeper community. Few people minded these announcements; in fact, they generated conversation later and strengthened community. Yet as the announcements grew more creative, they introduced an unpredictability to worship, especially regarding the length of the service.

In addition, I noticed that the other opportunity for unplanned congregational input was changing as well. Prayer requests were turning into small testimonies, as some people did not want to offer requests but stories about prayers that were answered. We were also beginning to hear more background on the prayer requests. The problem here was that people simply offered these prayer requests from the pews. The ministers would report back to the congregation the gist of what had been said, using the pulpit microphone, but much was lost in our summary. People complained that they wished they could hear the stories from the speaker, but the layout and acoustics of our church make this impossible. Still, it occurred to me that there might be a way. If we could encourage people to come forward to the lectern, they would be heard. There were too many prayer requests each week to make this feasible for everyone, but I wondered if we could occasionally single people out, and ask them to prepare to say something.

We had one member who gave a lengthy and beautifully crafted testimony each year on his deceased mother's birthday. The anniversary of his mother's death would lead into a few lessons she had taught him about faith and life and, one year, when the anniversary fell on Palm Sunday, the significance of that festival. I came to expect that this prayer request and the attendant lessons would be coming and to allow time for it, since it was well prepared, like a mini sermon. I asked him to deliver the request from the lectern rather than the floor, and it was well received.

For the third year in a row, people were telling me that they looked forward to our stewardship season, because they hoped to hear the members of the church offer "giving moments," which were, in effect, our first testimonies, I now see.

What happened with the giving moments was that people told stories about their walk with God through the life of our church. Sometimes they were funny. Sometimes people cried. As one member put it, "I love stewardship season because I get so excited about what people will say."

While no one would use the word *testimony,* based on what I saw happening at Church of the Redeemer, I sensed our congregation was hungry for the practice of testimony. When I presented the idea in early 2000 to the deacons (who are the lay leaders responsible for the worship and spiritual life of the congregation), they agreed.

People often characterize New England Congregationalists as stodgy and stuck in their ways. I recall the old joke: How many Yankee Congregationalists does it take to change a light bulb? Answer: Three. One to change it, and two to stand around asking, "So what was wrong with the old one?"

That old joke could not be further from my experience of the lay leaders at Church of the Redeemer. They were a remarkably open group, willing to try new ideas but also willing to scrap them when they did not work. I am convinced that this openness allowed us to experiment in a variety of ways that contributed to our growth.

In *Rerouting the Protestant Mainstream,* C. Kirk Hadaway and David R. Roozen offer a word of hope that seems to reflect recent growth at Church of the Redeemer. They write:

"For churches in metropolitan areas . . . great possibilities exist for growth and decline. Furthermore, urban churches appear to be more open to change than rural churches. It follows that it is easier for urban pastors and lay leaders to institute a process of revitalization."[2] But together as leaders, we had to be creative in how we introduced testimony, given the wariness of change in the church. While it has been carried out by Christians throughout history, it had not often appeared in the middle of worship at Church of the Redeemer—but we had hopes for the revitalization it could offer, based on the few experiences we had had listening to one another.

So we had to introduce the practice while honoring our own church culture. In 2001, it was the deacons who came up with the phrase "Lenten Reflections," sensing that these were words the congregation would understand. Then we invited five people we had not heard from before to prepare something for a worship service during Lent. But I knew we needed at least one guideline. And so, as the pastor, I laid down just one rule, which might seem like a silly rule unless you attend a mainline church yourself. The rule: Lenten reflections must not be Godless.

In *After Virtue,* Alasdair MacIntyre writes: "A practice involves standards of excellence and obedience to rules as well as achievement of goods. To enter into a practice is to accept the authority of those standards and the inadequacy of my own performance as judged by them."[3] If this was to be a Christian practice, our testimony was accountable to the tradition of Christian testimony itself. What could we testify to on Sunday morning that we could not just as easily testify to on National Public Radio?

As a minister and teacher of Christian practices, I didn't want Lenten reflections limited to subjects like "all the good that civic-minded people can accomplish when they work

together," or "why New Haven needs a stronger living wage
ordinance," or "what I have learned about myself in psycho-
therapy." But as long as God was in it, those things could be
too.

Our definition ended up being simple. A testimony was
your spoken story about how you had experienced God, offered in the context of our community worship. Trusting that
God would be in this, I tried then to keep myself, as the pastor, out of it. When members offered to show me their reflections beforehand, I told them that I trusted them and would
prefer to hear them on the same Sunday as the rest of the
congregation.

At the time I began to write, we had been using the practice of testimony in our church for over three years, long enough
for it to have become an accepted practice in our transient
population, where doing something three years in a row makes
it a tradition. We had moved the testimonies to different points
in the service, but usually we placed them in the first half of
the service, when the children are still with us, just before the
passing of the peace, when the children usually leave for Sunday school. From the beginning, we wanted the children to
experience testimonies too, since it was our custom to include
them for many significant liturgical events, from communion
to confirmation to sermons where appropriate.

We continued to invite and recruit members to give testimonies. Lay leaders (usually deacons, members of the church
council, or the financial development committee) or the ministers thought of people to ask, brainstormed for ideas, and
then approached the person directly. It was still not common
for people to volunteer, even though we called for volunteers.
But when we asked, almost everyone said yes, and often something like, "I have been waiting for you to ask me and think-

ing about what I might say." Some people declined one time but agreed another. When they declined, it was generally out a sense of shyness or the fear of speaking in public, and not out of an objection to the practice.

It is my thesis that the practice of testimony strengthened the bonds among us as a community and drew us closer to God as individuals and as a community. Yet there were many other transformations that occurred as a result of this practice. To put it simply, the practice of testimony drew us into a closer examination and understanding of other practices of the faith. You see, what I learned as a pastor is that the *practice of testimony* turned out to be *testimony about practices.*

In 2004, I left Church of the Redeemer to accept a new call. So in this book, I reflect upon eight years of ministry at a church I am no longer pastoring, but one that shaped me and shapes me still. As I looked back on how we grew into the practice of testimony at a mainline church, I have focused on three years worth of testimonies and found that they pointed to certain themes based upon the type of practice or transformation we experienced. There were obvious themes, such as those we deliberately set up when we asked people to offer testimony on money and giving or another specific subject. Yet even these testimonies then pointed to other practices as well, such as thanksgiving or honoring one's elders. Some clear themes and practices of the faith come out over and over again, and these are the ones I have written about in the chapters ahead.

There were also themes that I expected to find that never appeared. I had one preconceived notion about testimonies that proved false in my particular congregation. Specifically, the testimonies I had heard at other churches focused on the need for a personal relationship with Jesus and the Holy Spirit.

These topics were not raised at Church of the Redeemer, for reasons I will explore.

What follows in this book are some of the testimonies themselves, linked thematically with the practices they embody, and the ways in which our community experienced transformation. Included as well are reflections from those who have given and heard testimony. Without using the typical words of testimonies from another tradition, these Christians were reflecting on where they had seen or felt God at work in the world. From what I heard in their words, in each case, it was the practices of the faith that had opened their eyes. In the chapters that follow, you will hear how speaking about God's transformation transformed us as a church.

CHAPTER 1

The Household of the Heart

Throughout our experience of giving testimonies, we found that many of them referred to or depended upon other practices of the faith. But one strong connection ran through them all: the tie between hospitality and testimony. I have come to believe that hospitality is a necessary precursor to the giving of testimony, but in that first year, 2000, in the first Lenten season we shared our testimonies, it was the very first testimony itself that pointed me to the subject of hospitality, a theme that would remain vital for us as a church. The Christian call to hospitality—to welcoming the stranger into our midst and making of the church a household of God—this call led us into sharing more than our physical space. It led to us sharing our faith and welcoming one another into the spiritual households of our hearts.

The welcome began with a testimony from our moderator, the chief lay leader of the congregation, who had always been in leadership during my years there, and long before that. David is in his fifties, an architect with close-cropped hair and a reserved New England manner. I had assumed he was going to speak about a recent long-range planning leadership meeting, but instead he spoke about another retreat that had taken place four years earlier.

David

Lent 2000

I grew up in an agnostic household, where Lent was an exotic part of other people's lives. I'd like to relate a time in my life, much longer than 40 days, when I was in a kind of spiritual wilderness, cut off from connections between my true self and the people around me.

In 1983 at the age of 34, I came out as a gay man, first to myself, then to my family and friends. Loyalties were stretched, some toppled, most survived. I divorced my wife and struggled to find what it meant to be a gay father to our five-year-old daughter.

I was in church every week, singing in the choir, but not a member of the church—participating in but not connected to worship. I served on the missions committee, and when I was invited to serve on a search committee for an interim minister, I figured it would be a good time to join the church, but I was still in the wilderness.

One Sunday afternoon in August 1997, I was back in my office, working alone against a long-term deadline. There was a church leadership retreat at Lillian's home at 5:00, and for reasons I don't understand, I decided to go.

It was hot that day. I didn't feel comfortable with the people there. I didn't know what would happen. We started with a simple exercise: Lillian read a scripture passage about the transforming power of the Holy Spirit. Good stuff. Then she asked each of us to write about a transformation in our own lives.

I couldn't think of a "safe" example, so I wrote about the personal transformation I experienced in coming out, in accepting myself as a gay man. No one had to know: I was writing this for myself.

But when Lillian asked if anyone wanted to share their story, the Spirit moved me to volunteer. I didn't know what would happen. There was a lump in my throat, my palms were sweaty. I took a leap of faith. It was a leap back from the wilderness into a new relationship with God, one based on my true nature. It didn't hurt that no one gasped or avoided me; in fact, I felt affirmation. In moving me to speak from my heart, the Spirit had also transformed my relationship with the congregation.

I felt radiant, lighter than air. I felt that I had found home.

I hope we can learn together how to call others from the wilderness to a home in this church.

The Practice of Hospitality

After David offered his reflection, he rejoined the choir to sing the offertory anthem red-faced. I noticed people who were in tears, as there would be every Sunday during this first Lenten season of testimony.

My sermon that day was on spiritual practices, but I could have thrown it out and not preached; no one would have noticed because it would have been the testimony that they remembered. Visitors commented to me that they loved the worship service, which excited me, but in later weeks I would see visitors leave in the middle of worship, right after the testimonies. People are always wandering in and out of church, for any number of reasons, many of which have nothing to do with the church, but I found myself wondering if the testimonies were offending them. I began to wonder if we would need to monitor the effects of the testimonies. But how would we do that? Might we have decided at some point, "We are paying too high a price for this practice"? We had no system in place for evaluation, wanting the Spirit to move among us, but what if all this backfired? Testimony was going to turn out to be a risky practice.

The normally private David had set the bar high, with his honesty and the impact of his words. He had revealed himself in ways that were not common among New England Congregationalists, and from the get-go he had put out a challenge to those who would go after him.

I was particularly struck by what David said about the role other practices had played in his journey. I remember very well the retreat he described, and I remember when he read what he had written about his own experience of transformation. I was a new minister and the congregation was small, surviving but not yet thriving, and the leaders were tired. It had taken them 18 months to call me as their minister, after serious conflict between members and ministers and two church splits in recent decades. Now that I was here, the leaders wanted to rest. Raring to go after my first few months, however, I called a leadership retreat and decided to have it at my house. Sometimes people open up more in people's homes than they do at church gatherings, gradually making their way into the more intimidating atmosphere of worship. I wondered if gathering the church leaders at a home would make church feel homier.

In her book *Making Room: Recovering Hospitality as a Christian Tradition,* professor of Christian ethics Christine Pohl draws the connections between our various households and our faith, tracing them back to New Testament times:

> Households remain the most important location for hospitality in the New Testament period. Fellowship and growth in the earliest churches depended on household-based hos-

pitality among believers. For Greeks and Jews, the household (Greek: *oikos;* Hebrew: *bayith*) was very important and served as a basis for social, political, and religious identity and cohesion. For the early Christians, rooted in both Hebrew and Greek traditions, the church as the household of God was a powerful theological and social reality. The church was made up of a family of households, but it was more than the sum of those individual households. The church was a new household, God's household, and believers became family to one another.[1]

That day of the retreat, my small living room was full, and the store-bought cookies were shared like the loaves and the fishes. I hoped that after years of conflict, our church might become not a household divided but a household of God, as Pohl had described. David was not the only one to tell a dramatic story that hot day. A retired attorney revealed a radical change of lifestyle after a stroke; others spoke candidly about the church's past. Looking back, hospitality played a role in making room for a number of testimonies. Outside of the church meeting room with its ghosts of fights past, God did a new thing in someone's living room, and those stories that leaders shared were definitely testimonies in which they told me as their new minister, and one another, important things about themselves, our church, and God. In the formality of a church meeting room, it can be harder to be oneself, to be *at* home, as we can be *in* a home.

The connection between what happened in the living room and what later was able to happen at church was made possible through the practice of hospitality. It strikes me that in order to encourage testimony, you must first practice hospitality, so that speakers will have the sense that the words they entrust to the community will be valued and not denigrated. A community that practices exclusion would not have valued David's words that day, either in the living room or the sanctuary. Pohl makes the connection between hospitality in the home and in the church in the following way:

> Early Christian hospitality was offered from within this overlap of household and church. A homelike setting provided a natural environment for expressing personal qualities of hospitality. The church as a gathered community required the most immediate connection to God's character and expectations—behaviors suitable to the household of God.[2]

Pohl argues, as I would, that it is God's character to be hospitable and welcoming, and therefore the church should be too. If God in Christ welcomes all of us, we should welcome one another. But these steps of welcoming can take place in a variety of settings. Christians are called to a radical hospitality that is deeper than what is practiced at a VFW or a Scout meeting; we are called to love our enemies, not to cast the first stone and to welcome one another as God has welcomed us.

David had been a participant in the church long before that retreat. Originally, it was the practice of singing that had drawn him to the church and kept him there. As a musician, he had found his place in the choir, had been met with hospitality and shared it with others, and had been shaped by that practice even before he considered himself fully engaged. Singing had drawn him into God's presence, and then into the church.

When David said in his reflection, "I was in church every week, singing in the choir, but not a member of the church, participating in but not connected to worship," I believe that through the Christian practice of singing, God had been working with David all along, laying the groundwork for his later testimony, the practice that would result in his deeper involvement with the church. Still, there was no question, as David described in his Lenten reflection, that the welcome he felt that evening in my home was a new hospitality, a welcoming of him just as he was, that had not been present at the church before. I know that in this warm and small community, people had known David's story before that day, but I don't think he had spoken about himself publicly with the church, certainly not in the context of a leadership gathering or a worship service. The congregation didn't change that day; David did—by offering that testimony publicly and formally, in a church event. But then, over time, his testimony changed the community who heard it, connected us more, as it changed us again in worship when he told the story four years later.

Testimony seems to have no beginning or end, no alpha or omega. After we tell God's story, it tells us, and then we have a new story to tell. The stories shape the community, and the community responds with new stories. But both the telling and the hearing have the power to transform.

Hospitality ended up becoming a theme for our small congregation. Before we grew numerically, we grew spiritually through this practice. We started eating together more often, welcoming one another more warmly before church, and listening to one another in meetings. The people who joined appreciated this hospitality and practiced it after they arrived. Today Redeemer is known as a welcoming church, and the testimonies are a big part of what people appreciate. It is welcoming for a visitor to hear someone they have never met before share their faith in an honest way.

My observation has been that every church would say they believe in hospitality. They just don't practice it. It's the practice that makes transformation possible. But what allows us to start practicing what we preach? And what prevents us from doing it? Dorothy Bass and Craig Dykstra, in their work on practices, relate a lack of hospitality to fear. It is scary to welcome the stranger, to open up a circle of likeminded people to change, or even conflict. I found this insight very helpful as I have reflected on the ups and downs of the congregation's hospitality. What we first think is a matter of theory turns out simply to take practice. As I looked at our history of hospitality as a congregation, long before I arrived, our hospitality had always increased as our fear decreased. A church that thinks its demise is around the corner does not have the excess capacity to welcome the stranger. A church that lives out of scarcity is afraid to share. But as our congregation's fear about its future decreased, we were able to do bolder things, like offer testimony, change our worship patterns, and set up new programs. The more we opened ourselves up, the less power fear held over us.

This was my hope for those Lenten reflections—that in listening to a few people offer testimony, we would all feel less fearful about doing this in our everyday lives. What happened for us in hospitality might happen for us in sharing our faith. As we let go of fear, it would have less hold over us. And it ended up being so.

CHAPTER 2

To Join or Not to Join?

When people venture into a church community, from another tradition or after years away from institutional church life, one of the most confusing areas to them is how, or even why, to become members. Different churches receive members in different ways. Are you required to go through confirmation class all over again? Is showing up, attending, and pledging simply enough? When you move from one type of Christianity to another, is this a conversion? Or a betrayal of your past?

Pastors and long-term members of a local church often forget how confusing it is to sit at the edges of the circle, and wonder whether or not you are included, or whether or not you want to be. When I look back on our practice of testimony, I realize that an early decision, made unconsciously, proved to teach us a great deal about ourselves. From the beginning of our practice of testimony, we did not limit the testimonies to members but chose from among the members of our community, whether they were official members or not. This proved to be a window into a world in the church that I as a pastor did not know enough about. Many of the testimonies, it turned out, centered on the theme of whether or not to join the church.

23

Testimonies Told Us About Ourselves

In listening to the testimony of some people who were new members, and some who were not members, I began to hear a word of correction to the local church. While we might think our procedures on how to become a member are clear, in the testimonies of members and nonmembers, I learned that they were not. I also gained new insight into why some people join and why others do not, and the deep discernment behind such decisions.

In the Congregational tradition, similar to many other mainline Protestant denominations, newcomers attend, and then at some point are invited to make a decision as to whether or not to join. The invitation is seldom heavy-handed or even urgent. Perhaps they read that a new member orientation class is starting, or they meet with the pastor about a child's baptism and realize they ought to join the church themselves.

But in joining, they learn that they do not simply fill out a form or add their name to the parish register anonymously. They must stand up during worship one Sunday, and in front of the congregation make a verbal covenant. The congregation then, in turn, makes a covenant to the new member. This turns out to be a big decision.

If they are joining a Christian church for the first time, they will be baptized. But if they have already been baptized, in the new member liturgy, they repeat once again the baptismal questions, and recall the moment of their baptism as they join a new local church. Often, people who join a new church are transferring a membership from church to another. This is the case with many Protestants, who understand that when they join a new church, their previous church will be contacted to issue them a letter of transfer. A letter of transfer has the air of continuity. You are not renouncing one thing for another, merely transferring.

But for Roman Catholics the process is different, since the Catholic Church will not transfer a person's membership to a Protestant church. Furthermore, in many pastoral conversations, I have learned that for people who were raised Catholic, the idea of standing up in worship and joining a new local church feels strange. As a result, they might faithfully attend our church every Sunday, even pledge generously and volunteer their services, but they will not join, for joining our church would mean leaving another. To them, it would mean to stop being Catholic.

Given that Catholicism in Connecticut is such a cultural identity as well as a religious one, this decision to join or not to join the church weighed heavily. Class differences from the past would come up from Catholic family members who wondered why their son would want to go to a "WASP" church. Issues of ethnic identity emerged, as well as immigrant traditions. In New Haven, there are still presumptions that Italians worship one way, the Irish another, and in many families the decision to join a church not identified with one's ethnicity felt like a rejection of it. So some of these people attended a Protestant church, supported the community, but did not join out of a sense of loyalty to family and the past.

Sometimes this question of loyalty applied to people who were not raised Roman Catholic, but perhaps felt a tie to their family through another tradition. "Our people have always held their membership at the Episcopal church downtown," they would say, adding, "We'll come here, but we could never officially leave our old church!"

Or could they? As a pastor I have come to learn that these discernment questions about whether or not to officially join a church are very intense for people, and the church could do more to understand the many nuances of that discernment.

The reality is that whether they officially join or not, people from various other religious traditions are shaping and being shaped by new communities of faith all the time. In *Studying Congregations: A New Handbook,* this phenomenon is treated seriously, and the research conducted nationally certainly applied at the church I served. We dealt with a rich mix of people who turned up at our church, most of whom had no connection to the denomination but described themselves as "church shopping." Whether or not they stayed or joined, they were having an impact on the local church. *Studying Congregations* described it helpfully:

> Congregational cultures are constantly being remade and passed along to newcomers, whether intentionally or unintentionally. No congregation can count on its current members to last forever, nor can it count on a guaranteed pool of potential members from its community or even from its own progeny. Congregational membership in the voluntary system of the United States is neither prescribed by law nor inherited in unbroken line from ancestors. The last several decades have, in fact, seen a vast increase in the degree to which religious affiliation (including the decision not to affiliate) has become a matter of individual choice, a matter indeed of several choices across a lifetime, as people move about and switch from one religious group to another. All congregations then are faced with the ongoing task of integrating newcomers into the existing culture of the place.[1]

During our years of testimony, that issue of integrating newcomers popped up again and again, as did vivid descriptions of how people discerned whether or not they were called to be official members of the church. But it was an early testimony, during the first Lenten series, that introduced some themes that would become more important as we moved forward. That Sunday, two Yale Divinity students, an engaged couple in their early thirties, decided to do a testimony together.

They were enthusiastic to give their testimony, and expressed to me what a difference our church's hospitality had made in their lives. They appreciated our welcoming stance toward all people, and knew that that hospitality extended to leadership as well. New people were often given leadership responsibilities where they would serve alongside long-term members. Kevin was a good example of this. Raised Lutheran, he had joined the church a year before and was already on the board of deacons, entrusted with the spiritual leadership of the church. His situation is not unusual.

Our church like so many was a transient community, where experience was not, and could not be, a must for new leaders. In New Haven, graduate students who spend many years getting a Ph.D. end up being longer-term residents than the average corporate transfer, but few of them are there for good. As people moved in and out of town, we had so little time to instill practices of the faith, or to take time developing seasoned leaders, that we moved quickly. Sometimes that brought chaotic results, but many people experienced transformation. And as a pastor, I believe that the practice of hospitality in a congregation should inevitably lead to welcoming new people into leadership alongside long-term members and to enriching the church. It is not enough to offer people a cup of fruit punch after church and call yourselves hospitable. Real hospitality takes place when the newcomer is invited into ministry and decision making in the church.

And finally, I believe that another way to practice hospitality is to invite people to give testimony whether they are members are not. Sometimes when a church ventures into testimony, we immediately think of asking our more experienced church members to speak. But in opening up testimonies to the newcomer or the outsider, we may learn important things about our faith community and the discernment of those who wonder whether or not to join it.

In that spirit, two newcomers to the church, engaged to be married, one of them a new member and one of them not officially a member, one a Protestant, the other a Roman Catholic, offered testimony on the second Sunday of Lent as part of our first round of Lenten reflections.

Kevin and Kathryn
Lent 2000
Kevin

As a relatively new member here at Church of the Redeemer, it is easy for me to remember what led me here and what drew me to become involved in this community. When I moved to New Haven two and a half years ago, I was a person in search of a denomination. I had tried a few different ones on for size but had yet to find a place that really expressed the wideness of God's grace and the loving freedom of the Christian life—at least, as I understood them.

Much to my embarrassment, I had never heard about the United Church of Christ before I came out to the East Coast . . . so we might want to take this up with the publicity department! Eventually a friend at school filled me in on what the UCC was about, and so I decided to experience it firsthand here at Church of the Redeemer. You could say that I came for the polity, but stayed for the community.

What I found here was a group of people who (as Lillian has put it) live in some very creative tensions. There is a deep appreciation for tradition but also a commitment to invention and new ideas. There is a palpable sense of purpose and activity in this congregation, and yet also a sensitivity and attention to nuance. But more than any of this, I just got the feeling that here was a group who exuded God's care and love to each other. I think I got tipped off by the passing of the peace, since the version of it here is possibly the longest and most mobile that I've ever experienced! Whatever the reason, I sensed that this was a community in which I could connect with others and be involved in a very exciting ministry.

Kathryn

Before I began at the Yale Divinity School several years ago, a priest I was friends with told me he was worried that I might lose my Roman Catholic faith in the midst of so many Protestants!

At the time, I felt highly satisfied with my tradition and thought his fears were unfounded. During my years at the divinity school, I began to appreciate other traditions and see some of the faults in my own, but I still felt most at home in the Roman Catholic Church. Even though I disagreed strongly with my church's official positions on many issues—especially with regard to gender and sexual orientation—I could not bring myself to leave the church I grew up in.

I first came to Church of the Redeemer only because I wanted to participate in worship with Kevin. The more I came here, the more I was struck by how diverse this community is and how welcoming it is to all people—even struggling Roman Catholics!

To my surprise, I began to feel more at home here than at my own church. For the first time in my life, I had a wonder-

ful experience of worshiping God without laying aside any of
my convictions about the equality and dignity of all people—
whether man or woman, gay or straight, young or old.

Though I have not yet felt ready to take the leap of
converting, my experience of the worship and community here
have affected a very significant conversion within my heart
and mind, and I look forward to further exploring where God
is leading me.

Kevin

This last summer, Kathryn and I decided that we wanted to
commit our lives to each other, and so we've been talking
about weddings a lot recently. We've spent many hours
discussing what kind of ceremony would best express the
relationship to which God has called us. Should it be Roman
Catholic or UCC? Should it be sacramental or covenantal?
Should it be traditional or more creative?

Also, with our families spread throughout the country, we
had some location issues as well, and so we discussed the
possibility of having this ceremony at the various churches we
have attended in the past. But eventually we decided that who
we are, individually and as a couple, and the path God is
leading us on could be most fully celebrated here at Church of
the Redeemer. Moreover, we felt that New Haven is our home
right now, and that this is our church.

And so we look forward to celebrating a commitment
ceremony this coming August, right here, and we feel over-
joyed and honored to be able to participate in a worship
service that is inclusive and affirming of all God's people, and
that proclaims our love and commitment to be lifelong
partners.

Everyone should have to sit back and listen to newcomers
describe their community to them, as we did that day when

Kevin and Kathryn spoke. I delighted in hearing them describe the welcome they had felt with us, and winced when Kevin pointed out that no one had heard of our denomination. (What publicity department?) I heard those worries about abandoning Catholicism from Kathryn, as I also realized how much a congregation could mean to someone who had not chosen to join it.

Whatever we may believe about ourselves, what we project to the newcomer shapes our community. But sometimes we don't know what the newcomer hears us saying about ourselves. Listening to their testimony is one way to hear who it is that we say we are. Who we are depends a great deal upon whom we attract and whom we repulse. In listening to testimonies, we hear what is attractive about our community, and sometimes we hear about what needs fixing.

I was struck by Kevin's positive reaction to the "passing of the peace." In the Christian liturgy, the passing of the peace is a moment during the worship service when we stop to greet one another with a handshake or a hug, which is the sign of God's peace. The passing of the peace usually has strong proponents and opponents in any congregation. Some people love it; others hate it. Some churches hug one another; others offer one another a cursory handshake.

But at Redeemer, the passing of the peace usually lasted five minutes, sometimes longer. People did not just shake hands with those next to them, but choir members would leave the choir loft and walk down into the congregation. All over the church, people left their pews and walked around. It was indeed a moment of chaotic hospitality.

We usually timed the testimonies to occur just before the passing of the peace, so when a testimony had been offered, this time became an opportunity for people to greet the person who had just spoken. Thus the peace could turn into a time of "mini testimonies" as people said to the speaker, "Let me tell you about something like that experience you described that happened to me," or "I came to this church for the very same reason." The peace was a powerful time in that people took time to actually speak to one another. After Kevin spoke about how important that lively passing of the peace moment had been to him, many people told him that they experienced the same thing.

But then something unexpected happened after Kevin had spoken so fondly about the passing of the peace. Other people began to talk about it from a different perspective. For example, in one coffee hour conversation the day of the testimony, one newcomer told us that for him, the passing of the peace was a lonely moment. He told us that people seemed so excited to greet those they already knew, but in stark contrast only a polite handshake was exchanged with the newcomer. Kevin had raised the issue, positively, but it opened up a conversation about the practice, and soon others came forward and spoke of that same loneliness. His testimony was the first part of a learning that reminded us that the most important person to greet with the sign of God's peace was the newcomer. Often testimonies reminded us what we were doing as a church that was working and occasionally raised questions about what was not. Testimonies started conversations about life in the church that continued long after the Sunday had passed.

As communities of faith, we tend to hear from the ones who stay. The ones who leave may have a more critical story to offer, but do we care to seek out those stories? I must admit, I do not.

While some church leaders actively seek out the stories of those who do not choose to stay, I tend to think that those people's stories should be held and cherished by the community they eventually end up joining. I certainly would not open up a space in the worship service for a person angry at the church to speak. But I have found that listening to the testimonies of those who have recently discerned a call to join, or have not discerned one yet, can be fascinating.

In Kevin and Kathryn's story as a couple, we found two different stories about responses to that particular practice we have in the United Church of Christ of officially joining the church. We heard one story about a person who had said, "Yes," and the other from someone who had thus far said "No thanks" but might be in the process of saying "Maybe." It was a gift to be brought into their stories.

Kevin and Kathryn did not know it when they spoke, but they told the story of many couples in the congregation who struggled to bring together their two different faith stories into one worship experience on a Sunday morning. Kathryn described her Roman Catholic identity so strongly in the story about the Catholic friend who worried about her among the Protestants, but I had heard those sorts of words from several men who sit beside their Protestant wives in the pews more regularly than some of our official members. It seemed that about one half of the couples at Redeemer were struggling to accommodate two different religious backgrounds. Some interfaith couples simply worship separately; for example, one in a synagogue, one in our church. But when both are Christian, they have other options. Do they pick one branch of Christianity or the other? Or do they choose, as a couple, a church new to both of them? When the split falls along Catholic and Protestant lines, we often saw couples that attended our church together, but the Catholic person, like Kathryn, did not officially join.

There were many people at Redeemer who behaved as members did, pledging and attending, attending potluck suppers, Bible studies, and even the annual meeting, but were not members. It raises an interesting question: Does adhering to some of the practices of the tradition make you a member of a shaping community? Or must you engage in the Congregational practice of standing up in front of the congregation and making a membership covenant in the context of worship?

As a Congregational minister, I push membership. Membership matters, I tell people. It is important to stand up and tell the church you are committed, and it is important to hear the congregation promise to support you in your walk of faith. I find that if I wait for people to get there on their own, they never get there. These days, few people approach the pastor volunteering to join. They need a nudge. Even people who drive up to an hour to get there are still tentative. First we have to get through their suspicion of joining anything, their distrust of institutions in general.

As noted in *Studying Congregations,* our American religious system is purely voluntary. People do not feel obligated to join a church. But in addition, the generations that have followed the great generation of World War II are suspicious of institutions, church, and others. So when people wrestle with whether or not to join our local church, we are dealing with their issues around organized religion and institutions in general. Then, being Congregationalists who join by making a public covenant, we confront their understandable old-fashioned stage fright.

In general, our newcomers and visitors do not want to stand up and make a religious covenant in front of the whole church in the middle of worship. They would rather do just about anything else. Sometimes they negotiate. An unbaptized adult will ask to join the church, joining a church for the first time, without being baptized. This is not the practice of our shaping community, so I say no. I go back to pushing the importance of the public covenant. Kathryn's story reminded me why that pushing can feel so hard, even unmerciful. Her struggle, over wanting to remain Catholic, yet loving the worship and community life of our church, came through in her emotional delivery. Yet Kevin's delight in having taken that step reminds me why I do it. The fact that they both love the church reminds me that God's love in our community is not limited to our various understandings of membership.

A Testimony of Two Churches

Three years after this testimony came another, this one from a Roman Catholic man who had not joined the church but had been a part of our community for 17 years, along with his wife who was a member and had been raised Congregationalist. At the time of his testimony, Joe was serving as cochair of the Christian education committee and would have looked to any newcomer like a long-term member, but in fact he had not joined.

Churches have different ways of including people like Joe— the ones who come all the time yet have not joined. Our bylaws will often state that certain forms of leadership are open to all. For instance, at Redeemer, the bylaws said that you could serve on the Christian education committee and the missions committee as a nonmember, but you must be a member to serve on the board of deacons or trustees. Clearly our generation was not the first to notice that we had people who were not official members but still wanted to contribute to the leadership life of the church. Someone before us had in those bylaws made a way for nonmembers to serve. Yet that was perceived in an interesting way within the church.

Someone once said to me, "In our church you're not allowed to be a deacon if you're Catholic. Only Protestants can be deacons." What he was referring to was that you must be a *member* to be a deacon, yet I wonder if it felt to him like the old division between Protestants and Catholics from New Haven's history. Many of our deacons were raised Catholic and still vigorously claimed that identity, but at some point they made the choice to join this congregation.

But in that comment, for that person who had not joined and wondered why "only Protestants can be deacons," I saw that from his point of view, the church was allowing Catholics to do some things and not others. What we saw as a creative way to include nonmembers (on the education and missions committees) felt to him like exclusion (from the two other committees, the deacons and trustees). What might seem like a perfectly appropriate requirement that leaders be church members, felt to him like another Protestant elitist move to exclude a Catholic. Church policies are always seen against a larger backdrop of the community and its history, and in New Haven the history of divisions between Protestants and Catholics was still a painful one.

So against this backdrop, in the fall of 2003, Joe laid out in his testimony his own rich history with a well-known Roman Catholic church in town that had recently been torn down and merged with another church. The story of the demise of St. Peter's Church was a painful moment in New Haven's history, after all the church had meant to those who had been a part of it. Joe's description of his two church identities and his struggle with Roman Catholicism evoked an enormous response in the church. He offered his remarks as part of a testimony about giving, but they were about much more than money. They struck at the heart of what it means to belong.

Joe
Fall 2003

I first walked through those doors about 17 years ago. My future wife, Lorraine, had just joined this church, and I didn't know anybody here other than her. The church was nice enough, but I had been in plenty of nice churches and had been to a Protestant service or two. (I have been corrected a couple of times and told that Protestants do not have masses; they have services.) I had also decided that these services had one thing in common: they were all too long. I was used to walking into St. Peter's Church on Kimberly Avenue for 11:30 mass and walking out at the end of mass at noon. A 90-minute service here was the norm in those days. (Thank you, Lillian, for correcting that situation.) The Church of the Redeemer and I were not off to a good start.

Nonetheless, I kept coming back here with Lorraine. Not every week, of course. I still loved St. Peter's, even as it was falling apart around me. It was still a beautiful church. It was the first church I ever went to, the church that my mother and I used to walk to every Sunday when I was a little boy, right next to the school of the same name in which I spent some of the most wonderful years of my life. But I would find myself back at Redeemer on frequent occasions. There was something about this church, and the music certainly was good.

Then one day, 16 years ago, I married the girl of my dreams right here on this very altar. The entire ceremony took about 25 minutes.

Later, our children were baptized here. Lillian and Sam came on board as our ministers, and though there have been occasions when the views about current events expressed from that pulpit haven't necessarily agreed with my own, I began to get more involved with this church. I started attending coffee hour after services. Then I began to go to potluck suppers and church cleanup days. I found myself head coach of the Redeemer Dreamers softball team. I'm presently cochair of the Christian education committee. I'm on the space planning committee. I occasionally find myself at church council meetings, being an usher, teaching Sunday school. On more than one occasion I have turned to my wife and asked her, "How did this church ever get along without me?" Of course, just one look at the history of this church displayed in the tower lobby lets you know that this church got along just fine, thank you very much.

I don't tell you all of this for self-aggrandizement, but to drive home a point. I was never really active in any church before this one. I'm active now because this church is different, this church is special. Don't you see? Look around you. We don't all look the same, we don't all act the same, we certainly don't have the same political views, and many of us don't even live here in New Haven anymore. We come from all different directions just to be here. Here, at this church.

Oh, sure, the building itself is beautiful, the organ is one of a kind, but it's the things you don't necessarily see when you first visit here that make this congregation unique. It's our ministers whose sermons are never dull. It's our choir that's so good that some visitors think that we must pay them.

But most of all, it's you. You people sitting out there in those pews. You make this church unique. I know because a few years ago a couple of priests from outside the area and I had a little disagreement on what constitutes a good Catholic. I won't go into the gory details, but I will say that the episode was potentially devastating to me. But my experiences with this church, along with a heart-to-heart talk with Reverend

Daniel, assured me that God was with me. And he thought I
was doing OK.

They tore down St. Peter's not long ago—the church and
the school. To this day as I drive on I-95, I can't look over at
where that beautiful campus and those two wonderful buildings used to stand. I purposely avoid Kimberly Avenue. I guess
I should be able to find some solace in the fact that they at
least built a new school there, and it's not just a parking
garage or some overgrown weed-infested lot, but I don't. Until
the day I die, I'll always regret that there wasn't something I
could have done to save St. Peter's. All it would have taken
was money.

I heard George Carlin once say that God can do anything,
but that God always seemed to need money. God can perform
all of these wonderful miracles, but doesn't handle money very
well. Perhaps God doesn't need money, but God's church does,
because without the proper funding, difficult decisions have to
be made. Building maintenance takes a back seat, because the
electric bill needs to be paid. Services to the community get
cut, because the money's just not there. Family outings like
hayrides and snow tubing, outings that bring a church and its
members together, disappear. Attendance on Sundays begins to
slip, because as some members move away and others are
summoned to our Creator, visitors who come to the church
and would normally replace those people who have gone don't
bother to come back, because they see nothing special about
the church. And then one day, you look at a New Haven
Register, and right there on the front page is a picture of a
large demolition machine with its huge claw tearing down
your beautiful church and all of the memories that are inside
of it.

I'm not going to try and convince you that there's a
wrecking ball or a bulldozer in this church's near future, but

experience has taught me that once a church begins a decline, it's nearly impossible to stop. This church is growing. Even being in an urban area with no parking, it's still growing. Let's all help that process along. This community needs a church like Redeemer. Let's all make sure that it always has one.

Who am I to ask you to increase your pledge to this church? Nobody, really. I'm not officially a member of this congregation; I'm not even a Protestant. But I know something special when I see it. I hope that you all see it, too. Amen.

Joe's eloquent remarks brought home to me that while we may have category of "member" or "nonmember," God has no such categories for the people in the pews. Yet Joe reflected a concern that he and others must feel when he said, "Who am I to ask you to increase your pledge to this church? Nobody, really. I'm not officially a member of this congregation; I'm not even a Protestant."

But he went on to claim his authority and place in the church as one who recognized "something special," as one who had experienced God's grace in this, his community. For there could be no doubt of Joe's commitment to the people and to the church in his remarks. So many people appreciated Joe's words, and were so glad to hear how he felt about the church. Many also understood what it was to have lost the church of one's youth, whether by choice or through having it literally razed to the ground. This generated conversations that strengthened Joe's emotional connection to the church and created new friendships.

Five months later, when I asked Joe to reflect on how giving that testimony had changed him, he wrote:

> The one thing that stays with me about the entire experience is that my standing in the church seems to have changed. I've

always thought of myself as one of the church's "characters," but now I seem to be something else. Everybody seems to know me now (not always a good thing, because I'm terrible at remembering names), and I can't imagine myself going somewhere else to worship. That thought gives me both comfort and anxiety at the same time. Comfort because I have found a place that I love as much as any other church I have attended. I do indeed miss St. Peter's, but having Church of the Redeemer in my life softens the blow.

Joe had explained to us, without using the words, how the Holy Spirit had moved through our church, to somehow connect us to the church of his youth. His testimony reminded all of us that our definitions of membership and our categories are merely human, while true belonging falls under God's purview. There was no question that Joe belonged, and in talking about it, he belonged even more.

By belonging more, he also became more of a leader, later agreeing to serve on a key new committee of the church, the capital campaign committee. Lay leadership was strengthened not only for Joe but also for those who heard his story and saw themselves in it. They realized that people with backgrounds similar to theirs could play vital roles in a denomination and church they had not grown up in. And I suspect that in preparing his thoughtful words, Joe came to realize this about himself as well.

Testimony Brought Outsiders Inside

Looking back, that initial decision to invite both members and nonmembers to give testimony was made without much reflection, but it proved to be important. It raised for me, as a pastor, a struggle within the laity that I had not fully appreciated, as to whether to join officially or not. I also saw how useful it is to hear newcomers describe the church that others of us are familiar with. We are reminded of how we appear to others, and can either celebrate or correct as a result. And also, in allowing the newcomer to testify, or the outsider to testify, we begin to break down the walls that separate us and to learn that in our stories, we connect to God's larger story, and then connect even more to one another. While we human beings struggle with the divisions within the church, and wonder whether or not to join one tradition or another, we might remember that in God's story, we have already been joined, one to another.

CHAPTER 3

Money: We Need to Talk About It

One day I was driving along Whitney Avenue in New Haven, just outside my church in the neighborhood of Yale Divinity School. A van suddenly pulled out in front of a great big, shiny sports utility vehicle. The van jerked back just in time to avoid hitting the SUV, but the driver of the SUV screeched to a halt next to me. I watched the driver, wild with rage, jump out, slam the door, run up to the van and pound on it. The mother and the children inside the van looked terrified.

A string of expletives were the prelude to his chilling words, "You could have hit me! Do you know how much this thing is costing me?" Jesus lays out for us a way of life and a way of death. The man in the SUV did not even think to complain that the van driver could have injured him, a beloved child of God. His one thought was for the car and how much it was costing him. That car was costing him a price so high I suspect he is losing his life as he seeks to gain it. That is the way of death, and we are all touched by it in this broken world.

In my ministry, I am becoming increasingly convinced that salvation and conversion are not once-in-a-lifetime moments. They are ongoing surprises that yank us off the highways of our own making and onto the more wandering paths of Christ's peace. Once there, someone in need may find us, worshiping in our congregations on the weekend, yet leaving to be part of rituals and patterns of spending that cause them pain. What will they hear in our places of worship? In our church, I hope and pray that they will hear testimonies that point to the way of life.

Our testimonies began with what we called "giving moments," in which members spoke in church about giving to the church. These were offered during the stewardship season as a way to urge people to contribute, but soon turned into the highlight of the fall each year. At this early point, we preferred the term "giving moments" to "testimonies," but later that following Lent, we embraced the term "testimony" and went on to call them "giving testimonies" from then on.

We did have guidelines for our giving testimonies. Initially, we knew what we did not want. We did not want a "sales pitch," a "hard sell," or a "guilt trip." We did not want people pointing to the peeling paint in the sanctuary and telling everyone it was time to "chip in." We wanted these to be worshipful moments in which people spoke not of the church's needs, but of our human need to be generous, and to give. So the giving moments were opportunities to reflect on the joy of giving, on the theology of generosity, on the Christian practices of household economics. As such, with these kinds of guidelines, we were creating the space for testimony, allowing people to reflect on their experience of God.

Testimonies Cut through the Cumber

In *Practicing Our Faith*, Sharon Daloz Parks explores the following themes in her chapter "Household Economics," and uses the Quaker concept of "cumber" to describe the cluttered nature of our lives.

Many feel that the most we can do is simply keep up, managing as best we can. Our calendars are bursting, and we are busy; even children are busy. We are working more and faster, in part because the incentive structures in our present economy have a bias either toward long work hours or multiple part-time jobs. We work at these jobs to secure our sense of well-being, increasingly defined by access to the goods and service we need and want.

One consequence is what the early Quakers called "cumber." Billions of marketing dollars are spent worldwide to make a dazzling array of products and services attractive, even "necessary." Moreover, the market has become ubiquitous. Once we only *went* to the market. Now the market comes to us—to our homes, workplaces, and public spaces through television, telemarketing, magazines, catalogues, and online services. We wear advertising on our clothing and plaster it on every façade of our common life. And it works. Americans now spend more time shopping than citizens of any other nation, and we spend a higher fraction of the money we earn.[1]

Sharon Daloz Parks describes the culture of our congregation's members perfectly. Even those who are not wealthy can relate to this experience of cumber, of having too much of the wrong kind of stuff, combined with the sense that all this cumber is sapping meaning from our lives.

When I first arrived at the church, it had a tradition of two yearly rummage sales. Well-meaning people from church and the community brought in their cumber all year long, leaving cardboard boxes full of old books or clothing in the halls of the church. This left the entrance to the church looking messy on a semipermanent basis, but we felt we were providing a

valuable community service. Yet, the task of sorting out all
these donations, carrying them down to the basement or trip-
ping over them in the halls, preparing people's castoffs for
sale became onerous. Eventually, a community choir took on
many of the duties and split the proceeds with us. But after
these sales, our congregation was left with all the donations
that no one bought. Our undercroft would be full of junk that
often would sit there until the next rummage sale, until the
amount of junk was taking over the space. We would call
around to places like the Salvation Army or a homeless shelter, only to discover that they did not want this stuff enough
to come and pick it up. The process of disposing of the "cumber" from the rummage sale involved members using their
vans to give away stuff that had been given to us.

We discovered that cumber is a problem that cuts across
class lines in America. People of wealth and people without
wealth know what it is to have too much stuff that does not
satisfy. From forgotten toys to signs posted at the local dona-
tion site saying, "No, we do not want your old computers,"
to children who ignore their brand-new bike in order to watch
a TV commercial advertising the next thing they are going to
want—we are surrounded by evidence.

In *Plain Talk about Churches and Money,* sociologists Dean
Hoge, Patrick McNamara, and Charles Zech interview pastors on the subject of money and find many different points of
view, as well as a lot of pain. It turns out that many pastors
think they do not do a good job of teaching about money,
often because they themselves are not at peace with the subject. The same problems that plague church members plague
their ministers: consumer debt, fear of job loss in an uncertain
economy, the struggle over how much to give away to the
church when money is tight at home. When pastors them-

selves are uncomfortable about money, it becomes difficult for them to share the gospel critique, and so an awkward silence from the pulpit ensues.

In James Hudnut-Beumler's gem of a book, *Generous Saints,* pastors candidly debate whether they ought to know what their members pledge. Clearly, if the subject of money is taboo in the society, that taboo affects churches and pastors too. How much should pastors know about their parishioners' habits? The power of the taboo around money is particularly intense around issues of giving. If pastors do know how much their parishioners give, should the parishioners know that they know? All this creates more awkward silence, among the laity as well as the pastor.

It was these hard questions about money that lead us into testimony. Everybody wondered what to pledge, but nobody was talking about it. We had a feeling that there were people in the congregation who had something to teach us, but we were afraid to ask. We wondered if we were the only ones who struggled to make a family budget, and suspected there had to be help out there in our Christian community. Our giving moments were born out of our need as a church to hear from one another on these hard subjects, and to realize that we were not alone. But in practicing this type of testimony, we were being decidedly countercultural because we were breaking the cultural taboo that says we don't talk about money, and we were breaking that taboo in church.

According to professor Robert Wuthnow, in his book *Poor Richard's Principle,* what many people hear in church may not be very helpful. I am haunted by Wuthnow's story of former U.S. Steel executive William Diehl who says, " 'never in thirty years did his church (which he attended faithfully) give him any guidance in how to apply his spirituality to his work. . . .'

There was absolutely no connection between Sunday and Monday,'" Diehl says.[2] Diehl received no guidance about work, and yet his work had enormous economic consequence. We wanted, as a church, to do a better job of making the Sunday/Monday connection, and the subject of money was a way to begin.

I know that most Christian ministers are afraid to talk about money as often as Jesus does. It appears to be Jesus' most pressing topic, much more pressing for instance than the topic of human sexuality. Jesus speaks about wealth, and possessions, and embraces the poor over the powerful again and again. This angered the powerful, of course. We may follow Jesus, but we don't want to end up like him.

We certainly don't hit the issue as head-on as Jesus did when he said to the rich young ruler, "How hard it will be for those who have wealth to enter the kingdom of heaven." What does God think of our religions today, passionately splitting over issues of sexuality but united in a marked timidity on the subject of money? Ironically, you could say that on issues of money, the average congregation's position might be characterized as "Don't ask, don't tell."

In *Poor Richard's Principle,* Wuthnow examines America's moral history with money and makes the point that as a nation, we no longer apply moral principles to wealth; we simply accept that spending decisions are governed by market forces that are somehow out of our control. Liberal or conservative, Wuthnow sees all our churches as being complicit in not critiquing the market place. "It is wrong to think of the two sides as being engaged in a 'war' involving fundamentally opposing worldviews. The two agree on so many other things, and they have drunk so deeply at the well of American individualism, that they are often indistinguishable. . . . Neither side poses moral restraint on economic commitments with a very high degree of effectiveness."[3] For hope and guidance, Wuthnow points to alternative voices from New England's history, from the Puritan ascetic moralists to the romantic transcendentalists, to remind us that our nation used to have better tools for reining in the economic appetite.

For example, Church of the Redeemer was founded in the early nineteenth century by a group of Congregationalists who were profoundly influenced by the teachings of a Yale Divinity professor named Nathaniel Taylor, who is quoted by Wuthnow. Taylor was one of the ascetic moralists who did not fit the stereotype of the dour Puritan burdened by the Protestant work ethic. Taylor preached that people of faith ought to devote themselves to much more than their work. He urged people to "make some sacrifices of private interest for others' good by a largeness of liberality, and an extent of beneficence proportioned to your known ability."[4] Jesus puts it better in Luke 12:48: "To whom much has been given, much is required." This was the theme our moderator (the chief lay leader of the congregation), Marilyn, chose when she offered a giving testimony to the church.

Marilyn
Giving Testimony 2003
In the giving testimonies that we've heard so far this year, both Jane and Joe shared some of their faith history with us. So, I tried to think back over my church history. And I think I've figured out why, as an adult, I was drawn to the UCC and why I love Redeemer.

I was baptized at DeWitt Memorial Church in Lower East Side Manhattan. It was a nondenominational Protestant church and the members were black and white and Asian,

surrounded by a community that was predominantly Jewish.
My first experience of church was one of diversity in a time
when you rarely found diversity in America. When I was five
years old, we moved and my parents took us to St. Albans
Presbyterian Church in Queens, New York. That lasted until
we moved to Amityville, Long Island, where we attended St.
Paul's Lutheran Church for a few years, St. Mary's Episcopal
Church for a few more years, and finally Hollywood Baptist
Church. Summers I spent in Virginia with my grandparents
where we attended revival meetings all over Buckingham
county each Sunday. We'd spend all morning in church, then
share dinner on the lawn—fried chicken, potato salad, deviled
eggs, collard greens, and sweet potato pies—and then the
grown-ups would go back inside for more church all afternoon. We kids got to play outside in the afternoons. At those
revivals, there was shouting, testifying, and ladies dressed in
white to help those who fell out when they were overcome by
the spirit. By the time I was 16, I'd been a participating
member in four denominations and one nondenominational
church and a host of fundamental revivals. In high school, I
studied abroad briefly with a traveling school chaperoned by
Catholic nuns and brothers. Wouldn't want the Catholics left
out of my religious smorgasbord.

By the time I reached adulthood, my notion of what
makes a Christian community had at its core the idea that all
of God's diverse people should be welcome. It was this longing
for a Christian community that is welcoming to all people,
that is diverse in people and ideas, that attracted me to the
UCC and brought me first to Doc Edmonds' Dixwell Church
and then finally here to Redeemer.

And, I love Church of the Redeemer.

- I love the sermons—and not only those that I can agree
  with. I love the sermons that force me to think about

stuff from a perspective that I might not have considered. I love the sermons that tweak my conscience and complicate my thoughts.

- I love the music here at Redeemer. I love listening to it, I love rehearsing it, and I love singing it.
- I love the Upstairs Parlor—the first time I was ever in that room was when my extended family gathered there just before my mother's funeral.
- I love this old pipe organ that we're going to crawl around in later today.
- But like I said, most of all, I love the community of faith that we have become here at Redeemer. We have a fellowship here that is truly countercultural. I've read that 11:00 on Sunday morning is the most segregated time in America, yet here at Redeemer, we are living our commitment to diversity.

My love of Redeemer drives me to commit my time, my talents, and our money to the work of this church.

You know, last year, Alan and I were moved to increase our pledge for the third straight year, despite the fact that our income had decreased over the same period. There were times this year when we weren't sure whether we would be able to make good on that pledge. But then, an unexpected source of income presented itself and we were able to catch up on our giving. And I think that's one of the reasons that pledging is important.

I know that some of you give generously to the church, and yet you don't pledge anything. Pledging is important because it allows us to prepare a budget. I know you're all aware how important that is. Anyone who has to work on a family budget knows that it is difficult to plan your expenditures if you don't have a good idea what your income is going to be. Pledging allows us to take a look at the programs that we'd like to do, and decide what we can afford. It allows us to challenge ourselves to make the missions line items one-tenth of the total budget, something we did for the first time two years ago. This makes us a tithing church in our outreach.

But most of all, I think, pledging is an act of faith. It means saying, "I don't know what the year will bring. I don't know if we will have the income to make good on this pledge. But, we're willing to commit ourselves to the church and its mission and to take that leap of faith that our pledge represents." I told you that we were not sure whether we'd be able to make good on our pledge this year. Well, if we hadn't made any pledge, we would never have seen the unexpected wind fall for what it was—God making good on God's covenant, God's pledge to us. Jesus taught that everything you need, our God will provide. If you haven't pledged, consider pledging this year. If you have pledged in the past, consider increasing your pledge. Have faith.

What I found in the many testimonies that our church has had around the subject of giving, and therefore money, is that moral discourse on money can be so much more than Wuthnow's two dim views of the church—either the evangelical guided tour of Disneyland or the liberal relativism of sherry-sipping inner peace. I see in my own congregation's historical roots an opening to a future where those historic voices, such as those of our spiritual founder Nathaniel Taylor, can help us do better than that. And I also am filled with hope when I have heard the thoughtful insights members have presented in their giving testimonies. Marilyn's words were clear and forthright, as she talked about her family's income reduction and their increased pledge. She spoke concretely and honestly about a hard subject, but used that to move to the larger faith questions as she shared some of the rich details of her own history.

Giving testimonies were often rich like this—it's no wonder people looked forward to them.

As we listened to giving testimonies over the years, what I have been most struck by is how holistic their approach has been. The speakers may prepare themselves to speak about money, or a possible capital campaign, but what comes out is a full story of faith that generally begins or ends with the church. I don't think they were avoiding the subject of giving to the church but, like Taylor, they see their lives as a whole, wrapped in God. And so a testimony about increasing one's pledge is connected to the church of one's youth, to the economy of the day, and to the community in which we now worship.

Ethicist Sondra Ely Wheeler, in her book *Wealth as Peril and Obligation,* carefully reminds us that there is not only one scriptural message on the subject of money but a whole variety of stories. Perhaps each story and parable is a new word in the vocabulary for wealth that we need to develop. One word does not sum up Jesus' teaching on wealth, but a discussion using many words gets us closer to God's story. For some people, the struggle is to get rid of wealth and to give it away. For others the struggle is to more fairly distribute the world's wealth so that they too can eat. Jesus spoke to different people in different ways about wealth, because at different points we need to hear different things. Testimony within the body of Christ is a way to get people out of the concrete cumber around them, and to look instead to the real wealth of the Holy Spirit for a new way of being.

Nathaniel Taylor reminded his nineteenth-century students, "Leave no ground for the suspicion that you have not another and a better spirit than the world around you."[5] To our cynical ears, that call to see the holy within the ordinary world seems awfully bold. As Wuthnow points out, we tend to think the economic world is a natural order that we cannot affect, when really it is just another construct. The economic world is not like the weather, something that happens to us. We, as societies, shape it and are shaped by it. We can choose to behave differently, to spend differently, engage in the political process differently, run our workplaces differently, and perhaps bring more of Jesus' teachings into our lives, so that Sunday and Monday are not so distinct.

As people of faith, when we offer one another our testimony about money, we avoid the devil's trap of separating the material world from the spiritual world, and acknowledge the ways in which they are knit together. God is just as present on Monday as on Sunday. You can find God at the church, in city halls, or on the picket line. But we are the only ones God can work with to make those connections between our cities and the city of God. In our testimonies on giving, we helped one another make those connections over and over again.

Perhaps the owner of that SUV, the one with such road rage, will worship in our congregation some weekend. Perhaps he will hear a testimony from a fellow traveler. Perhaps there, in the middle of worship, he will suddenly realize that it was the car that owned him.

It takes a new pattern to break an old pattern. While the world offers its patterns through the never-ending call to have and buy more, the church can offer new patterns, such as a call to give more and to receive more. In our testimonies, we talked to one another about money through the lens of the gospel, and offered one another the hope that we are more than what we own. We did need to talk to one another about money, and in talking about money, we found ourselves talking about God.

CHAPTER 4

The Gift of Time

While people in our congregations suffer in a world of cumber and worry about whether they have enough money, they would most likely say they lack something much more precious than things; for example, time. Churches compete for people's time, in a world in which it is the one thing we cannot seem to make more of.

So naturally, one of the obstacles in getting people to agree to give testimonies was their own perceived shortness of time. "I'd like to give a testimony, but right now is just not a good time." I hated to think that testimonies would be another painful addition to someone's "to do" list, but in some cases, that was just what the testimony would be.

But after offering testimony, these same busy people would often have great epiphanies. Later they might tell me that the time they spent preparing their words for Sunday morning were the first peaceful, meditative moments they had had in months and that they were so grateful for the push to look inward or to stop and hear the still, small voice of God. As part of preparing the testimony, often the busiest people would reflect in new ways about how they had been spending their time and how they thought God was calling them to spend their time in the future.

John offered that kind of testimony—words that spoke to the heart of dads who run their kids from one practice to another lesson, two-career families trying to raise children and serve the church as well, people who rush from one task to another never feeling they did the last one completely or well.

But John took us in some unique directions and into a deep part of his own story as well. As one who was at first too busy to prepare his words, he discovered that in taking that time, the Word prepared him. For John, the testimony became a sort of Sabbath, where time stood still and looked suddenly different.

John
Lent 2000

This Lenten reflection is about the current 40 days and nights and the Advent season before last Christmas.

If you remember, a recent study found that America's youth were overweight because they were watching too much television and drinking soda. (Don't tell my son I said this; he'd be mortified.) Really, that article spoke to me, so I decided to give up television and soda for Lent. If you know me, these are no small temptations, especially during March Madness, the NCAA college basketball championships.

It turns out it's not as difficult for me to say no to these things as to face how I use my time or how I sometimes waste it. I'm a teacher, and I bring my work home with me. I coach at school, I volunteer to recycle most nights at school, and I take Johnny to hockey practices and games. I go to meetings. Like most of you, the list is endless.

As many of you know, my younger son, Drew, is low-functioning autistic. Since his diagnosis five years ago, my wife and I have spent a lot of time taking turns, one of us trying to do things with Drew, the other doing other things that need to be done in our lives. You can see how precious time should be.

What I have pieced together about myself over the past few years is that the mindless clicking on of the TV and trips to the fridge, or many other devices I have found to escape my reality, stem from a helplessness that I grew up with—helplessness with alcoholism and divorce in my family, and helplessness that I feel now, in not being able to help Drew express himself. In some crazy way, I have dealt with the guilt and frustration by turning it on myself with late hours and . . . the disappointment of not being able to do some of the basic things I need to do each day with my time.

So when Lillian gave the sermon during last Advent about being on God's time and handed out the purple ribbons, that sermon had a profound effect on me. (I'm still wearing the ribbon.) It is a slow process, but there are more times each day when I think of God. I had always thought faith would push itself through to a person no matter what you were doing with your time (or mind or body). God is all-powerful, but I learned you must meet him halfway. You must practice your faith, not try to fit it in around other things in your schedule. So I spend more time with Drew on his terms instead of trying to fix him. He's probably on God's time more than most of us. Let him fix me.

A couple of weeks ago, Lillian talked about how powerful it would be if we all prayed twice a day. Since this Lent season began, I have tried to think of God the last thing before I sleep and the first thing when I wake. I pray a lot more, although it needs work. And you know what? Without some of the late hours of caffeine and video images, I have started remembering my dreams again and writing them in my prayer journal that I got on one church retreat. I consider my dreams a form of prayer and one of the Holy Spirit's ways of guiding me. Again, it is a slow process, but I am grateful to this church for helping me forgive myself and see my time through more faithful eyes.

Keeping the Sabbath

John was the last person I expected to give a testimony on the practice of faith. I didn't think he'd have time to engage in these things. I think we ministers often set the bar too low. It turns out that John, one of the busiest people in the congregation with some of the most difficult claims on his time, was the perfect person to lay out practices that help us value time.

Time seems to me to be the second most urgent pastoral crisis congregation members' experience, after money, and the two are so intertwined. They are at the heart of the most common reasons we give for not being what God wants us to be. Baseball practices and low bank account balances are frequent excuses for avoiding the very practices that might relieve some of the pressure.

John could epitomize the frenzy, but in his Lenten reflection he was a pilgrim on a journey toward deeper understanding. While there are chunks of time during baseball season when we do not see him or his son Johnny at church, and while John never mentioned the word *Sunday*, the practice he was describing was about honoring time, and that takes us into the practice of Sabbath keeping.

Historian Dorothy Bass lays out the promise of this practice:

> Whether we know the term *Sabbath* or not, we the harried citizens of late modernity yearn for the reality. We need Sabbath even though we doubt we have time for it. As the new

century dawns, the practice of Sabbath keeping may be a gift just waiting to be unwrapped, a confirmation that we are not without help in shaping the renewing ways of life for which we long.[1]

People are hungering for wisdom on the subject of time. Sabbath is not the only unwrapped gift we have waiting for us in the Christian tradition. As we rush from one appointment to the next, the liturgical seasons also remind us that God's calendar is more nuanced and graceful than we imagine. By introducing another calendar into our lives, the church raises the provocative question of who invents time.

God, of course, invented the entire created world, and in doing so invented time itself. How striking that even then, in the creative act, even God took time to rest and in doing so gave us the Sabbath. We were created to give some of our time to God as a way to remember that we do "manage" time. Rather, time is God's gift. Sometimes we have to take a break from our own busyness and creativity in order to recognize time as a gift, and to discern whether or not we are being good stewards of that gift.

The previous Advent, I had spent three weeks preaching on valuing time as an unearned gift from God. At the beginning of the season, we handed out small purple ribbons and asked people to tie them to their watches or their date books. Purple is the color of the Advent liturgical season, and the church is decorated in that color to remind us that the season has changed. So the ribbons were a way to take that reminder out with us into the world, and to remind us that in Advent, time is revealed as yet another of God's creations.

Time is not our God, but God is the Lord of time. For in Advent, Old Testament prophets predicted a birth that we today know has already happened. In the Advent worship services each week, we all act as though we are awaiting something that, of course, has already come to pass. Advent is all about unraveling time and reminding us that in its mystery, time belongs not to us but to God.

I had wondered if people would wear the purple ribbons. As a minister, I had thought that the ribbons would be a less intimidating conversation starter than ashes on one's forehead at the beginning of Lent, but I wanted conversations to start nonetheless. Looking back, I was trying for testimony again, wanting people to speak to one another about their faith and at the same time wondering if the possibility of being asked to testify would turn people away from the practice.

What happened surprised me. Not only did people wear the ribbons, but after Advent had ended, they refused to take them off. They liked having something concrete, a physical reminder. By the time John delivered the Lenten reflection, John's ribbon on his watch was ragged. The prayer journal that he had started at a retreat over a year before was a tool I had forgotten about but one that he had held on to. In Lent when I asked people to pray twice daily, I also sent them home with a bookmark that laid out morning and evening prayers. Some people needed no such guidelines, but I knew that others might need something to hold in their hands as well as the words to say. I heard this in John's testimony. Concrete objects play an important role in Christian practice.

John, a math teacher and an athlete, cares about the physical world so passionately that he spends his free time recycling paper, cardboard, cans, and bottles in all the communities he is a part of. Things matter. As ministers, we can forget about people like John. We can forget to link ideas to things that people can touch and hold and see.

Furthermore, when it comes to practices around time, the secular world is all too ready to provide things—handheld tools that promise order. The FranklinCovey Planner offers the illusion that we can plan anything. The Palm Pilot even offers us the ability to steer time itself, as a pilot. God has slipped from the dubious position of being my copilot to being a passenger on a busy schedule I am supposed to be piloting. An ad for *The Christian Century* several years ago showed an entry on a Palm Pilot screen that read, "Check out Christian Century." When I saw the ad, it occurred to me that the Palm Pilot might also have shown a slot reserved later in the day to check out God, before we go to the gym and after we attend a time-management seminar. But of course God is more than one of the items on our "to do" list. God is larger than any list we could come up with, and should be the backdrop against which we view all those activities.

Tools to "manage" time abound in the world, but they don't solve the problems. They don't address the painful fact that for human beings, time feels scarce. The Christian tradition offers practices and symbols to remind us that the liturgical calendar is not the same as the world's, to remind us that God's time is larger than our time but sometimes the Holy Spirit just breaks in with a disruption in the schedule that makes us see time in a new way. Testimonies were often like that for us. They seemed like another thing to do, just as coming to church can sometimes feel like just another thing to fit in. But then we hear a word, a testimony from one who struggles and has learned, and we may, on a busy morning, receive a gift of time.

CHAPTER 5

Honoring Our Elders

In testimonies, we found a way to draw people together. A long-time member would tell a story that drew the newcomers into a shared history. Similarly, newcomers described the church they were finding at this moment and drew the long-term members into their reality. And while not all the long-term members were older than the newer members, the newcomers did often represent a younger generation. Testimonies then offered our church the opportunity for some crossgenerational conversations.

Often testimonies became a chance for church members to offer tribute to one another. Sometimes a testimony would involve a story about someone long gone from the church. Other times, someone would refer to someone in the pews and the way that person had taught them. Testimonies became opportunities for people to honor one another as well as God. These days, when so many of us do not live near our extended families, many people are deprived of the crossgenerational relationships that would have been taken for granted decades ago. But church continues to offer that gift, and so the testimonies became a mechanism by which the younger members could speak to and about their elders, or the elders could speak about the younger members, and in doing so they could honor one another.

So often, one generation in the church feels ignored or unappreciated by the other. This could be set off, for example, by the pastor's age. If the pastor is young, as I was, and the new members are younger than the current members, as they were, the older generation can begin to wonder if the church will still have a place for them. Combine this with our culture's worship of youth and discomfort with aging, and we can see why the older generation in churches might resist the changes younger generations bring. One way around this is to engage in the practice of honoring our elders in the church.

One Sunday in our first year of testimonies, my husband described two elders of our church in his testimony. He was inspired to speak about these two men after visiting with them while they were sick. He had been visiting with one man to read to him, a custom that he had dropped during a busy spell, and then recently resumed. And he had called on one man in the hospital, which was the event that inspired the testimony below. The Christian tradition has always called upon us to care for the sick. In this case, that led a young man to honor the elders of the church, and share with the congregation some thoughts about living and dying well.

Lou

Lent 2000

Good Morning, Brothers and Sisters. This morning I would like to talk about learning from the old lions. I want to talk about the spiritual guidance I have received from older men, and in particular one man in this church, the Reverend Ed Edmonds, whom many of us call "Doc."

The relationships between fathers and sons can be very tricky. Because we must wade through so many layers of meanings—anger, pride, rebellion, grief, pity, humiliation—the love of fathers and sons can be confusing. I think that is why it's a good idea to have grandfathers.

Both of my grandfathers were wonderful, generous men. Flawed, I'm sure, but since I knew them only when I was a child, I still hold them in dream-like perfection in my mind's eye.

Anyway, I suspect I've been hunting surrogate grandfathers my whole life. I'm interested in how men can age with grace, courage, even elegance.

A few months ago, Newt Schenck ended up in the hospital. As most of you know, Newt is a pillar of New Haven, a remarkable civic leader, and a sporadic attendee of Sunday services here at Church of the Redeemer. I swung by Newt's room at Yale–New Haven Hospital, where I am working to organize a union. There was a sign on Newt's door that said that he was tired and to check with his nurse to see if he would take visitors. He agreed to see me, so I went in and he said, "How nice of you to come by. What can I do for you?"

I told him that the hospital police had been chasing me down the hall, and asked whether it was OK for me to hide in his room.

We laughed a bit and then settled down to a long, lively conversation. Matters local and international, the future of New Haven (a city we both love), the great attributes and great flaws of our mutual alma mater (Yale), the hopes and perils of the biotechnology industry, the history of the labor movement—we talked and talked. I had to tear myself out of the room.

I felt that God had given me a gift that day.

Shortly after that visit, I resumed reading for an hour or so each week to Doctor Edmonds, who sits here most Sundays as our own rather elegant prophet. Visually impaired since he was a young man, Doctor Edmonds has a brilliant mind. But even more, he has a lion's heart.

Doc is a nationally known civil rights leader. He had his life threatened during the fifties and sixties. He built a black middle class in New Haven. The stories are endless. The clearest picture that I have of Doc is from the winter of 1995–96. Yale was trying to significantly weaken and perhaps destroy our unions at the university. We had endured two month-long strikes. Three hundred people—union leaders, community activists, and a few clergy—committed civil disobedience on Grove Street in the middle of campus and refused to clear the intersection. When the police reached Doc, they refused to arrest him. I remember Doc fighting, really angry, demanding to be taken down to the jail and processed with the other protesters.

In short, I am a student of Doc. I have watched Doc, and I have learned. I have learned about life, and I have learned about God.

Here is what I have learned about life from Doc:

- Read, read, and keep reading.
- Raise strong daughters.
- Temper your anger with humor, but stay angry.
- Paint your dreams with large brush strokes.
- Have strong opinions.
- Spend time with younger people even when you feel horrible, and as your health wanes and the tethers that hold you to this earth get looser and looser, realize that from your new height you have an even bigger vision to share with those of us still tied to the ground.

Here is what I have learned about the liberator God who Doc and I both worship.

- God challenges us to engage in struggle.
- God asks us to sacrifice.

- God asks us to carry heavy burdens.
- God sacrificed God's only son to redeem our broken world, and compared to that pain and sacrifice, we don't have to do very much.
- Fight to bring about God's kingdom of justice and peace.

I pray for myself and the other young men of this church, that as we age we can follow in the footsteps of the old lions— fighting for what we believe in, giving strength to those around us, and pointing the way to God's kingdom on earth.

Testimonies often reminded us that what we as churchgoers have done over the centuries has been done for a reason. Visiting the sick and caring for the infirm reminded Lou that when he visited these elders, he had a chance to learn from them. The visits shaped him, as had these men's lives, and he used his testimony as a chance to talk about that. He honored his elders.

As Lou, at the age of 34, stood up and spoke during the church service, it was clear that he was doing what other young men had done before him. He was looking at lives well lived in order to understand what he wanted his life to be. He was turning to older men in the congregation for spiritual guidance. In the practice of testimony that day, he talked about what these men had taught him about God—and about that life-giving way of life. But he wouldn't have received this insight outside the basic Christian practice of visiting the sick when they cannot come to the church.

Lou's visit to the hospital reminded him of his lapsed custom of visiting and reading to Doc at his home. Practices seem to feed into one another. One practice reminds us to try another. But at the heart of this Lenten testimony was healing, not just the healing of people's bodies and not just the healing of the spirit that comes from being honored and listened to.

As Lou laid out his own search for new grandfathers, it was clear that he was searching for healing in his own life as well, not in the sense of seeking cure, but seeking wholeness. As a union organizer, Lou saw himself as working for a better life for the workers, and for a more just society, one that would be pleasing to the God of justice. He wanted healing in a broken world.

Lou and the men he spoke about all believe in a healing that will encompass the whole community. It is not enough for only a few to live well. We all need to be made whole. A civic leader, a civil rights activist, a union organizer—these three men were not passively waiting for that healing, but believed that God calls us to be instruments of that healing. At different points in their lives, two retired and one at the beginning of his working life, they all still believed that the wholeness comes in the struggle.

So while both of these elders suffered in their bodies, they spoke with Lou less about the healing of a body but prayed also for the larger healing, for that healing of the nations. Therefore it seems natural that conversations about the state of our recession-strapped city and the fate of the labor movement would take place in a tangle of IV tubes and heart monitors in a hospital room. In the practice of healing, we pray that the community will be healed and that we will all be whole.

Yet questions of bodily healing were still present. As Lou, a healthy marathon runner and father of young children, looked at Newt and Doc, he confronted the betrayal of their human bodies and the inevitable betrayal of his own. What healing can unravel Crohn's disease or Parkinson's when sickness takes two old lions and knocks them down with pain? For Lou, part of his testimony was to confront his and their mortality, by understanding their lives, listening to their stories, and then telling those stories to others. Their testimony became his testimony; for example, when he described a God who is both his God and Doc's God.

We long for the knowledge that we, in these scarred and personal bodies, have mattered to God and will continue to matter to God as we go into the practice of dying well. When Lou talked about the lessons he learned, he said, "Spend time with younger people even when you feel horrible, and as your health wanes and the tethers that hold you to this earth get looser and looser, realize that from your new height you have an even bigger vision to share with those of us still tied to the ground." We don't talk about sickness and suffering very often in the presence of those who may be going through them.

In society we do not talk about "tethers to the earth getting looser" (i.e., the process of leaving this life), but only about "getting better" from what ails us. Yet Lou had spoken to the men about failing bodies, and their words had mattered to him. He admired their courage and their ability to remain engaged with life even as their bodies let them down.

Doc was actually in church to hear Lou's testimony about him. As the Parkinson's changed Doc day to day, this Sunday when Lou spoke was the first time the congregation had seen Doc in his wheelchair. Doc's presence in the church gave an urgency and honesty to Lou's testimony that made us all uncomfortable. But I believe we were also relieved that someone was telling these men what we all wanted to say. Their leadership, as well as their illnesses, mattered to us all.

In healing and caring for those whose bodies grow weak, we have to look at mortality and loss within the body of Christ. As people of faith, we can aspire to more than to die and disappear. We are bolstered as we approach death with the promise of eternity. Yet the pain of losing a beloved member of the body of Christ remains. Newt has since passed on to that eternity, and at his funeral, in our overflowing church, many testimonies like Lou's pointed to Newt's engagement in civic life, a struggle for a better community, and the pursuit of shalom. But how remarkable it is when that testimony can take place for the living, not in the context of a funeral, but in the midst of Sunday morning worship and in the midst of life.

Perhaps Lou was anticipating loss. Perhaps he was anticipating a time when these men would no longer be there to know what they meant to him. So testimony provided a way for a younger man to honor his elders. Testimony opened that door.

When Lou gave his testimony, he was noticing the divine ground underneath him. Under our illness and our health, underneath fatherhood and great-grandfatherhood, underneath running a marathon or whatever is the next race that God has planned, the ground has been flattened by the heels of the generations who ran it last. Testimony is a way to acknowledge that holy ground.

CHAPTER 6

Making Connections

Testimonies often surprised me, but none more than Tony's. He told a story about how the wider church—and how one minister in that church—had changed his life. Tony used the practice of testimony to tie together some of the loose threads of his life story and to publicly thank a man to whom he was grateful and in doing so, taught us as a church about how the ministry of the wider church could change individual lives. It just so happened that the retired minister Tony wanted to thank, his former pastor who now attended our church, is one of the two "old lions" that Lou focused on the testimony from the previous chapter, and so we continued in honoring that elder as we made new connections.

Tony had a different story to tell, a story Doc had never heard before. Tony had always wanted to tell Doc about an incident from his past but had never found the words. So when I was approaching people about whether they would like to offer testimony, Tony approached me and asked to have a date to give testimony. "I have a story I have always wanted to tell," he said. "I want to say thank you to Doc."

Doc is a well-known minister in the United Church of Christ, the former pastor of Dixwell Church in New Haven, one of the oldest and most prominent African American churches in the nation. Doc joined our church after retirement, and several families from that church switched their membership around the same time. Tony's family had been at Dixwell, and was now deeply involved at Redeemer, with Tony serving on the board of deacons.

I had expected to hear a few words about how Doc's ministry in New Haven had shaped Tony's life, but I never expected to hear the twists and turns of this story. It would turn out to be a story that made remarkable connections between the members of the church, the local church and the denomination, church-affiliated schools, and one young college student's experience of the civil rights movement. Tony gave his testimony an unusual title that summed up what he would say—a reference to the work that Christians do to build the kingdom here on earth. He called his testimony, "A Little Piece of Heaven on Earth."

Tony

Just about every one of us has a perception of heaven. It is encouraging for us to believe that at some point after death, God will reward us for our good deeds. For me, one of heaven's rewards will be to know all of the answers to all of the world's perplexing questions. Questions like: Who was actually responsible for the assassinations of John F. Kennedy and Martin Luther King Jr.? Did NASA really place a man on the moon back in 1970? Is God a man . . . or a woman? Yes, real mind-benders. And God will provide me with all of the answers.

Well, to be truthful, the Good Lord has enabled me to experience a little piece of heaven on earth . . . while alive! You see, I attended Elmhurst College, a small suburban, coed, liberal arts college just outside of Chicago. Elmhurst was and is still a college affiliated with the United Church of Christ. This meant very little to me at the time, because I had been raised a devout Catholic. Yes, the alter boy, the Catholic schools . . . the whole, holy nine yards. Yet there I was, about a thousand miles away from my strict father and without any external restrictions. Oh, boy! The large church with the white steeple in the center of campus was significant only as the huge building that dwarfed the far more important gymnasium.

But I was not alone at Elmhurst. There were a significant number of new black inner-city students arriving on the Elmhurst Yard from all over the nation with me. We numbered more than twice that of the total returning black student enrollment. It seemed that Elmhurst, a school of staunch German domination and located in one of the nation's most affluent suburbs, had made a commitment to integration (we call that diversity now). And that apparent commitment was during one of our nation's most turbulent domestic times, just on the heels of the racial riots in the cities, and in the midst of the emergence of the Weatherman, Black Panther, and SDS factions on campuses. In fact, the Sunday that I arrived on the Yard was the day that Mayor Daley's police were busting the heads of the protesters at the Democratic National Convention. What a time!

We, the black students, were trying to identify ourselves; however, there were no proven role models—no modern, respectable role models. Not at Elmhurst. We struggled with the administration for recognition. We felt intimidated by some of the conservative white fraternities on campus. Many of us were athletes, and therefore we refused to run away. Instead, we gravitated to one another for support and for survival, becoming a community within the student body on the Elmhurst Yard. Within our community we had our distinct groups of mutual interest, and thus we struggled among ourselves. But in spite of all of this, we recognized an invisible, undefined power behind our being at Elmhurst. No member of the administration would admit that there was any outside influence requiring our presence.

But we sensed something.

Yet our investigation techniques were not sufficiently sophisticated to discover the source of the power.

We were being watched. The same recognizable individual who was always present when we were in groups was watching us constantly. After numerous complaints to the administration about that individual that were supported by pictures, the surveillance ceased. Or at least we thought it ceased.

We then figured that the power behind our being at Elmhurst was financial. We were all financial aid recipients, and therefore our presence brought government dollars to Elmhurst.

We continued our struggle and eventually the administration began to listen to us and to make positive changes to the curriculum and to the services. The changes continued through our graduation.

I returned home to Baltimore and began to work for Gulf Oil, married a devoted schoolteacher, and began a family. Gulf relocated my family to Connecticut, where I traveled the state marketing to service stations, and my teacher wife began teaching in the New Haven public school system.

We had both been raised in the Catholic Church but had strayed from that hierarchical dogma as we matured in college; however, we were ever spiritual and God loving—we just did not like the hierarchy. In Baltimore, we had visited a nondenominational Unitarian church that featured a noncharismatic, realistic preacher. So in our search for a New Haven area church to visit, we were attracted to the Dixwell Avenue Congregational United Church of Christ. The minister preached a positive message void of clichés. He was educated in the civil rights struggle, and he advocated for the disadvantaged. The congregation was active in the community and sought to be productive. We enjoyed their fellowship. After a long period of visiting, we sought membership.

During our membership qualification interview by the pastor, we divulged our history. It was during that interview that the pastor indicated that Elmhurst College was a United Church of Christ institution. I recollected that the insignia on the Dixwell UCC sign was the same as the vaguely familiar insignia on the sign of the large building that I remembered dwarfed the Elmhurst College gymnasium. I then became more explicit in my detail of my life on the Yard. The pastor listened intently, and when I finished, he began to relate to us how he and Rev. Cobb, along with other UCC ministers, had spearheaded the denomination's Commission on Racial Justice. It was the commission that was responsible for negotiating the funding to UCC schools that mandated the enrollment and the support of significant numbers of qualified black students at United Church of Christ colleges during the late sixties and early seventies.

EUREKA! The answer!

There I was, sitting in the presence of the person that was responsible for our enrollment at Elmhurst College. At that time I knew that God had provided me with the answer to one of, if not the most significant, questions of my life. What a shame that I no longer knew the whereabouts of any of my former Yard residents. How I longed to brag and boast to them that God had provided me with the answer!

The Reverend Doctor Edwin Edmonds, retired, Pastor Emeritus of Dixwell Avenue Congregational United Church of Christ and presently our own revered Church of the Redeemer member, whom we all know as Doc, was one of the primary individuals responsible for my enrollment at Elmhurst College. He was the Power!

Now, I have thanked Doc privately for the good work that he had done to help me in particular and to help so many in general. Many of those he helped implored upon his sense of obligation because they were the sons and daughters of friends and parishioners.

But Doc, you did not know me, nor did you know any of my Elmhurst colleagues. You had no obligation to help us. And until you met me, you were not aware of the maturation of any of us. To my knowledge, none of us had anything to do with Elmhurst College after graduation. Thus no accurate statistical data documenting the fruit of your labor at Elmhurst is available. You could only have faith in the belief that we would develop into positive, productive, good people, simply because what you did was right. I hope that over the years of our knowing each other, you have come to the satisfaction that your right has begot right. And in that, like me, God has enabled you to realize a little piece of heaven on earth. Thanks, Doc.

Tony's testimony was powerful to the congregation for many reasons. His description of his experience as one of only a handful of African American students at a private school, and the racism he experienced, rang true for other members of our church and sparked many conversations about institutional racism and the challenges to it. Furthermore, Tony gave voice to what many in our church felt—the frank admiration for Doc, an elder who had helped so many people in his academic and ministry career. Tony's testimony opened a door for many people to honor the man who had been their pastor and to teach this new congregation about the kind of man he was. The sharing of this story strengthened the bonds between the former Dixwell members and the long-term Redeemer members, as well as other new members, many of whom had not known Doc at the prime of his influence.

But Tony's testimony had theological content as well as a pastoral focus. He was speaking about the Christian call to do good without expected recognition and reward. Doc never met the students for whom he had fought, until late in his life, and his example was comforting for those of us who struggle for noble goals, only to wonder if any of it makes a difference. Tony's story was a way to tell his fellow Christians that their good deeds were making a difference, even when they wondered what had become of their work. Tony was a living testimony to that point.

It was also remarkable to me that Tony did not know who Doc was when he joined the Dixwell church and that it was only after attending and deciding to join that he made the connection. Tony was drawn to the principles underlying Doc's ministry, the same principles that had caused him to fight for those scholarships to enable black students to attend a church-related college. How remarkable that Tony would then discover the role Doc had played in his life and that Doc would finally meet the anonymous person that he had helped.

Finally, in a time when church-related colleges seem to be only distantly related to the churches that founded them and so many people have little connection to their own local church's denomination, Tony did some important teaching to the church. Many members have no idea that our denomination has a history of starting schools around the country or that there are still colleges affiliated with the United Church of Christ offering education and formation from our tradition. Tony's testimony generated conversations on that topic and curiosity among the members who wanted to know more. Many of them asked Doc about the history of the program Tony had described, which in turn gave Doc the opportunity to continue his ministry among us as a wise and experienced elder.

In Tony's testimony I was struck with the wealth of material that lies underground in our congregation's faith histories. Tony was one of the rare volunteers to give testimony. If we had not had the practice, he would never have had this opportunity to show his gratitude to Doc, to the United Church of Christ, and to God for all he had received. He would not have had the chance to tell us what it was like to be an African American student under surveillance at a mostly white, church-related school. He would not have had the chance to tell us how an altar boy ended up a Congregationalist with a heart full of Christian gratitude. Tony had been carrying this story around in his heart, looking for a public place to tell it, and his church provided him with that opportunity. His testimony connected the various threads of his life, wove us together more tightly as a community, and connected us to our wider church's history. Testimonies make connections.

CHAPTER 7

Preaching and Testimony

In February 2002, just before Lent began, I met with my professors from Hartford Seminary where I was pursuing my doctorate in ministry. In an oral exam, I was telling them about the practice that was blossoming in our church. It was a fruitful meeting in many ways, as I described the way we were using testimony in worship. But the moment I remember most vividly is when one of my professors asked me, "Have you given your testimony?"

At first the question seemed absurd to me. I was the primary preacher, after all. I would like to think the church hears my testimony week after week. But of course, they do not. They hear me preach every week, which may or may not include testimony, depending upon how personal the sermon is. This question by my professors led me to tease out the differences between preaching and testimony.

In my masters of divinity degree at Yale Divinity School, I had of course studied preaching, which is the proclamation of the good news of Jesus Christ. Was testimony the same as preaching? To my mind it was not. In a testimony, we can reflect upon our experience of God, or Christ, or the Holy Spirit. But in preaching, we begin with a specific biblical text, which is the basis of the sermon. The preacher's personal experience of God may be a part of a sermon, but it doesn't have to be.

Preaching may include testimony, but some preaching is not testimony in that it may not refer to a personal experience of God. This consideration also led me to realize that in the traditional sense, I had not actually given the congregation my testimony. I had not ever really told them my faith story. I wondered why I had not done so.

On the second Sunday of Lent, the gospel text was the story of Nicodemus asking Jesus about being born again. The Holy Spirit moved through our church structures as well as my resistance. The text offered the perfect opportunity for me to share my own experience. So why didn't I want to do it?

I believe it was because my own faith experience had a certain "born again" quality to it, a type of religious experience that might be associated with more evangelical churches but was not touted in the United Church of Christ. We associate such things with the conservative churches, and as such eschew such stories.

Yet my own experience might not be accepted in more conservative churches, for while it had felt like a salvation moment, I believe that my salvation in God's eyes had occurred long before that, perhaps even outside of time itself. And yet I had experienced it as a "once in a lifetime" moment. So in a sense, my own awkwardness in sharing my own experience with the living Christ was based on the fact that my born-again experience had no obvious ecclesiastical home. It didn't seem to fit the congregation I was serving, and bore little resemblance to the experiences the church members had shared thus far. I worried that in sharing it, as we began this journey of testimony, my story might have the effect of turning them off.

So in considering this, I came to an epiphany: while I had had the personal experience of feeling saved and believed my life had been transformed by it, my current ministry was not centered on bringing that experience to others. Certainly I spoke about transformation and about a personal relationship with Jesus, but I spoke about it theoretically, from a position of educated aloofness, as something we all ought to have, rather than speaking about it emotionally and personally, as something I did indeed have. I had not, in fact, given my testimony. And so I was determined to do so.

The sermon that follows tells the story of the tension in our United Church of Christ churches around testimony, and the tension within me, even as I was encouraging other people to stand up and do what I had not yet done. So the sermon begins in theory, with the larger questions, but moves finally into the personal.

Reading this sermon in retrospect, with its flaws and clumsiness, I value it because it appears to tease out the difference between preaching and testimony. There's an obvious point in the sermon where I stop doing one and move to the other. I stop reflecting on the biblical text as a minister and move into telling my story, one Christian to another. And when I did it, I felt the same fear that my church members had told me they felt, and then that same exhilaration as I sailed through my own small story, carried on a wind of tradition.

No Stupid Questions
A Sermon based on John 3:1-17.

Remember when your teacher used to tell you that there are no stupid questions? Good teachers say that to you.

Bad teachers do the opposite. Bad teachers say things to students like, "I can't believe you're asking me that. You know it's not lunchtime yet." "How many times do I have to tell you? That's not how you do long division. I can't believe you're still asking me that." (This is a touchy subject for me—as one of those adults who still mixes up long division.) Sometimes the bad teachers even say, "What a stupid question," or the more socially acceptable, "That's not relevant." You can just picture that little child's brain shutting down as the child becomes afraid to ask the questions that might lead to real learning.

Good teachers are the opposite. They want the questions. They say, "There's no such thing as a stupid question." They encourage their students to ask the obvious thing, because they want to know where the gaps in learning are, where the holes are in their teaching, so they can patch them up. Besides, the stupid question can turn out to be the deep and complex thing.

I always loved those teachers. They taught me one of life's great truths: it's a mighty fine line between deep and stupid.

Nicodemus was a Pharisee, a kind of intellectual Jew who came from a group that prided themselves on their knowledge. This was a group within Judaism that valued tradition and understanding—of the sort that puts the brain ahead of the heart.

Today, I would suggest that we still live in a world that can produce a lot of people like that. People who want to know it all but perhaps don't want to experience it all. Know anybody like that?

Pharisees were not bad folks; in fact, they were known to be pretty decent. Today, they'd be good experts, the people who appear on the news commenting about everything from the neck up. The type who describe deaths in the battlefield as "collateral damage."

Not bad people. But careful. The Pharisees were followers of rules, because they didn't see the value in everyone flying off into their own mystical experiences because that might make God cease to be God. They were cautious, wary of spiritual emotion and ecstatic religious experience, lest we all start creating God in our own image.

Sometimes I suspect that the Pharisees would have made good Congregationalists.

But Nicodemus, a Pharisee, knew Jesus had the presence of God with him. He had seen signs and miracles, and he began to wonder if there was a religion out there big enough for all he was feeling. But still he was afraid of what the others might think, so he came to Jesus late at night, to let Jesus know that he was getting it.

Jesus must have thrown him when he said, "No one can see the kingdom of heaven without being born from above."

"What?" Nicodemus asked. "Finally I get my courage up to sneak in at night and talk to you about what I feel in your presence, and you tell me I need to be born again?"

There must have been something gentle in the way Jesus looked at him because Nicodemus just kept going, throwing Jesus what sounded to us like stupid questions. "Can one enter a second time into a mother's womb and be born?"

It's a stupid question to those of us who understand the Christian tradition of new life and being born again, right? I mean, we all know Jesus was speaking in metaphor for the transformation in this life, right? We know what that means.

"No one can enter the kingdom of heaven without being born of water and spirit."

Or do we actually find ourselves joining Nicodemus in asking, "What on earth does this mean?"

This passage and the words that follow, "For God so loved the world that he gave his only son so that all who believe in him may not perish but have eternal life," are the heart of the Christian faith. John 3:16 was a famous verse long before the strange man in the rainbow wig started holding it up on a sign at football games. But do we understand it?

The early Christians seemed to see it this way. They came to know Christ, literally and in person, and their lives were changed forever. They were baptized at the moment that they felt the call of the Holy Spirit, and after that they were new people.

The traditional theological word used by the church to describe that moment is "justification," that moment of knowing that you are fully loved by God and saved through Christ's power.

The change that your life goes through afterwards is called "sanctification." The idea is that this experience is not a blip on the radar screen, but that salvation, or conversion, changes you. You are no longer the same—you are a new person.

Now, that reading I just gave you was heavily born-again Protestant. But historically, as the church developed in the Roman Catholic tradition, baptism came to be performed on infants, whose parents made promises on the children's behalf.

Did you know that today, being born again is not emphasized as a life-changing moment in the Catholic tradition? Some would say that much of Christianity has turned away from this doctrine, joining the mother church in baptizing infants

Yet many Christians are in "born again" Protestant churches, such as Baptist or evangelical churches, where only adult believers who have had a conversion experience may be baptized. No infants. And in every service there is an altar call from the minister so people can come forward and "get saved"—and getting saved matters in that tradition. Without being saved you forfeit eternity.

That idea is beautifully described in Dennis Covington's memoir, *Salvation on Sand Mountain,* about his journey from being a born-again Southern Baptist to becoming a Charismatic Christian snake handler.

He begins his role as a journalist, watching a small group of Appalachian Christians who believe that one of the marks of being born again is that you are able to handle serpents without being harmed, as described in the book of Acts. At the height of religious ecstasy, they drape themselves during worship in poisonous cobras and rattlers, and they believe you haven't really been born again unless you can do it too. Covington, a *New York Times* journalist, moves from observer to sincere participant, and in his book we are all reminded of the true diversity that is the Christian experience and the pursuit of the kingdom of heaven.

"No one can enter the kingdom of heaven without being born of water and spirit."

Covington describes how one church tried to live that out. Now, how about us? How do we live out Jesus' words? Even though we don't call people forward to get saved in the middle of our service, can we be born again too?

As in many things, our church and this denomination tend to walk down a middle road. You see that in baptism. Here in our church, in the United Church of Christ, we baptize infants, toddlers, and adults. You see that practice played out in worship on various Sundays, for you must be baptized in order to join the church. In this church we are hesitant to say that we have it all figured out, and we stand in between groups of Christians with opposing views and look for the commonality of our faith.

Some people would say that is wishy-washy. I'd say it's respectful of the mystery of God. And we also follow Jesus, who was far from dogmatic himself.

Still, the issue of new life in Christ haunts me, because having said those nice things about our United Church of Christ tradition, I will now say that I think we dodge this born-again language. In general we Congregationalists dodge the power of the Holy Spirit. We don't talk about lives being transformed. In that sense, we are good Pharisees.

But there's a rich tradition in this born-again language that we can lay claim to without saying that we know God's mind.

The Christian understanding of that moment of being born again goes something like this, and there are plenty of examples of it in the New Testament; for example, Paul's conversion on the road to Damascus being the most powerful. You are overwhelmed, perhaps with a sense of remorse for what you have done wrong in your past, and you ask God for forgiveness and feel it come to you in a powerful way. And then you ask Jesus to take hold of your life, and there's a moment of surrender—and then a sense of being saved. And after that, life is different. Not perfect, but different.

New life. It haunts many of us who were raised in the church. If you grew up Christian—with a few breaks perhaps during the college years when we tried being Buddhist, Quaker, New Age, whatever—if you have always been Christian and sit here in a Christian church as you have before, how do you define that moment of being born again? I don't know that we ever really will understand it fully in this life, but let me step away now from the theorizing, and give you a little testimony.

When I was 21 years old, I thought I knew it all. I had graduated from college, was working in a well-paying job, and looking ahead at what I thought my career would be in advertising and marketing. I had a great place to live, a new car, money to spend, and my whole adult life ahead of me. I knew and had it all.

And then my father had a heart attack. It's the kind of tragedy we all go through, but it hit me as if I was the first human being ever to confront the mortality of my parents. I visited my father in the hospital, and lying there in his hospital gown, he hadn't seen me come in. And so before he could put on a cheerful smile, I just saw him as he was, and he looked so terribly frail. The strongest man I knew was headed into angioplasty, seemingly shrouded in physical weakness.

Suddenly it hit me. I didn't want to be the 21-year-old only child of a divorced man, the only one to speak to doctors or to keep track of details. I didn't want to be an adult. I wanted to be a child again—to reenter that world where parents lived forever and only children are allowed to get sick.

After cheerfully kissing him good-bye and wishing him well, the way people do when they're pretending things are fine but certain they are not, I found myself wandering the halls of the hospital lost and crying. Embarrassed, I ducked into a chapel, and finding it empty, I went up to the little kneeler and lay down my head and cried.

That little church felt safe to me, like the only place in that medicinal building where people were allowed to feel, where you could just be sad, and I cling to that understanding of church even today. Church can't be just happy all the time, because it has to encompass the complexity of life. So I knelt there and soon found myself praying. It's funny how church can do that to you. And what I found myself praying was this: "What you have lain before me God, is too much for me. I am not the person you seem to think I am. How can I be a source of strength for my father when I am not a source of strength for myself?"

And I had this deep sense of not being worthy, of not being spiritually prepared for real life, for I had been living in the world of my own short-lived accomplishments, which works just fine until real life hits. I felt deep remorse for the shallowness I lived with and the distance I had traveled from God. And I asked to be forgiven.

And as I knelt there, I suddenly felt this tremendous peace, this sense of a blanket being wrapped around my shoulders, a sense that everything would be all right. I had this sense that Jesus was standing right behind me at that kneeler, with his two hands resting on my shoulders.

And then suddenly, I could see the whole scene, as if I were above myself, looking down. In seeing Jesus, looking so very sad, like a person who suffered himself, I realized that my father might or might not make it, and that the peace I was feeling was not the promise of a trouble-free life.

But it was the power of the Holy Spirit that could take a world of pain and put the balm of God over it. And in that moment, looking down at myself, I had the strongest sense that my life was not my own—and that my father's life was not his own. And that if I could relinquish the power I thought I had over my life, I would find a power greater than any other.

So I surrendered.

I remember the words going through my mind: I surrender.

In my young yuppie dreams of worldly success, the word *surrender* was the worst, but it sat comfortably in my heart that day. And I said, "I surrender my life to you, Lord. I'm giving my life to you." And I felt Jesus take it.

Now when I look back on that moment today, the debates about when one should be baptized seem awfully small. The debates over who is given salvation and who is not seem awfully arrogant. But I understood in that moment what it was to be born again.

And while it didn't happen in the church I grew up in, but in a hospital chapel instead, I know that my Sunday school classes and the scripture I had learned and the practices of the Christian faith had all been laying this quiet little foundation for the moment when I would need it most.

As far as being born again goes, I suspect it's not a once-in-a-lifetime thing. I've had moments like that since in my life, mostly at the times that I was in crisis about what life was throwing my way.

You've had those moments too. I know you have. And your testimony tells me you have felt the presence of God even there, especially there.

So when I hear Jesus' words, "No one can enter the kingdom of heaven without being born of water and spirit," I do not believe that my friends of other religions will be excluded from heaven. That's not what that passage means to me. I trust in the wideness of God's mercy. For, "Indeed, God did not send the Son into the world to condemn the world, but in order that the world might be saved through him."

What that passage tells me is that through Christ we will all be saved. But in our baptism into the Christian life here on earth, it's our lives here that will be changed. We do have new life. With that foundation in the walk of faith, we will see glimpses of that kingdom here on earth when we need it the most.

We will know that our lives are not our own. And that even though life will be hard, and the world can be full of pain, "God so loved the world that he gave his only son so that all who believe in him may not perish but have eternal life." Amen.

Preaching out of my own testimony was a wonderful experience—*after* the fact. But as I prepared to tell the story and wrestled with the theological questions of being born again and where they fit into our theologically inclusive denomination, I was nervous. I also came to realize why I had been drawn to the practice of testimony in the first place.

Within our denomination, I miss the freedom with which other traditions, especially born-again traditions, discuss their encounters with God. I have my own evangelical yearnings, my own saving experience, but a marked distaste for the politics of exclusivity that often gets thrown in with that theological expression. Could we mainliners, with a vision of inclusivity, also offer the excitement of saving testimonies about a personal relation with Jesus? I believed we could, but I had been asking lay leaders to do this without really having done it myself. I now understood their nervousness but also the elation of release afterwards.

This sermon received an enormous response, not all of it positive, but certainly lively. Many people pinned me down, demanding to know just who I believed was to be saved. I also heard a number of stories from people injured by the church and who worried about too much born-again language. But mostly, I felt that people sensed, as I did, the point at which I stopped preaching and teaching and started testifying. They understood that I was trying to meet them in the practice I had invited them into and were grateful.

I came to understand just how hard it can be to stand up in front of people and testify, and here I had been preaching and ordained for 10 years. It was hard to describe an experience of the divine to a large group of people, hard to share something so personal and so hard to describe. I came away more impressed than ever at the laity's willingness to try this practice, to fly without a net and allow God to do a new thing. I had felt that sense of vulnerability up there that day myself.

In turn, I believe this experience shaped my preaching. When I taught preaching at Yale Divinity School, I noticed that most seminarians were overly focused on themselves in their preaching. It was as if God could never have time for the rest of us, what with all the Almighty has done with seminarians' summer chaplaincy experiences. I urged students to not make themselves the heroes of their own sermons.

But in making my testimony part of my sermon, I was reminded of the place of personal testimony in proclamation. There is a way to preach authentically, in which the focus is on God, and yet personally, so that the sermon draws people in but does not make the preacher the faith all-star of the game. While we as a congregation became more comfortable with testimony, I believe I also came to share more of my own beliefs in sermons and to speak more about my own faith experience. I was freed up to do this, because I did not have to worry that listeners would think I was always raising myself as the one model or exemplar. Once testimony had been introduced, I could be confident they would hear something new and different, and perhaps more inspiring, another week from another testifier. The church's practice of testimony shaped my preaching and continues to.

In addition, I perceive that it shaped the preaching of our other minister as well. Our associate minister went on to give his testimony, but interestingly, he chose to give it from the lectern rather than the pulpit, and he did not offer it as part of his sermon. He seemed to be making a distinction. He did it in exactly the same way, and the same place in the service, as the laypeople did it. Sam told us in rich detail the story of his adult conversion, as a college student at Columbia University attending Riverside Church. In his testimony, he spoke about what had drawn him to the church, the intellectual and literary pulls of a critical approach to Scripture, and how much he cherished the liberal Christianity of that particular congregation. He spoke eloquently about the freedom of thought and the open theology of that intellectual church.

Sam and I differ theologically, and it was in his testimony and later in sermons in which he too began to include more testimony, that this became clearer to the congregation. It was only after we had introduced testimony that people began to approach me with questions such as: "I noticed that on Good Friday, Sam preached a really different message than I think you would have preached. Was he disagreeing with your last sermon from Palm Sunday?"

The person asking the question had in my opinion gotten it right. We were preaching somewhat different theologies. But I told her that it wasn't that we were arguing or disagreeing, but rather we were having a conversation within the rich and wide Christian tradition. The person's question was an opportunity for me to convey my respect for my colleague, and my trust in him, and for the two of us to represent what we as a congregation believe: that we do not all have to march in theological lockstep.

Sam and I had an excellent relationship as colleagues and would never put one another down or argue seriously in public. But it was also well known in the church that he and I saw the world differently. The key here is that we both saw that as a good thing, and I hope we conveyed to the church that our differences make each of us better ministers. One person would be drawn to one of us, and we were able to meet different needs as a result. Sometimes it was through our testifying that people in the church were inspired to raise something with one of us, out of that particularity.

I think it would be disastrous for a church to listen to two ministers in conflict turn the preaching event into an extended debate week after week. What I lift up here is that both ministers feel free to testify to God's power out of our own different experiences and do not feel we have to censor the theological differences. The congregation sees modeled in its ministers the respect for difference that our church upholds.

As the associate minister and I became more comfortable hearing testimonies and testifying ourselves, it has affected both of our preaching styles, in that both of us spoke more about what we had experienced of the divine. We spoke more from our hearts, when before we had spoken out of our heads. We shared more often a personal experience of God: our testimony. And as we have heard the rich diversity of the testimonies of our church, some of them sounding fairly evangelical while others quite Unitarian, I believe that Sam and I became more comfortable espousing some different theological visions from the same pulpit. I count this as an unexpected but rich blessing of introducing the practice of testimony into our church.

The church members noticed these subtle differences in our sermons and how they felt free to tell me, "Sorry, I'm with Sam on that one," or to say, "Why don't either of you ever preach on this subject?" or, "I look at it this way." By opening up the church in the practice of testimony, I believe the congregation is more attuned to the fine points of theology in testimony and more willing to weigh in. It is as if by inviting members to make their own testimony, each person can listen more attentively when others make theirs. And as we ministers listen to their testimony, they shape our preaching as well.

In hearing how my congregation described God, I learned where they were experiencing the holy, and also where they were not. I heard stories about how God had moved through events in our church that for me had been ordinary or even dull. And other times, I longed to hear them reflect on the Holy Spirit at an event that I had cherished, only to be disappointed by its absence. But in listening to their testimonies, I was guided in my preaching and in my leadership of the church. Testimony is very much a conversation, sometimes between the ministers and the congregation, sometimes between the ministers, and sometimes between those who have gone before and those still yet to come. In testimony, nobody in this life gets the final word.

CHAPTER 8

Children and Youth

In regular meetings with Courtney, our director of Christian education, I had spent time explaining the nature of my Hartford Seminary project to her, discussing the idea that the children might be included in this. Courtney, a bright and gifted teacher, was receptive. Her own leanings toward allowing children the freedom to ask questions and to express them connected naturally to the idea of testimony.

As a parent of two children in her program, I knew that whatever Courtney was doing downstairs was fairly close to testimony, because my five-year-old daughter periodically asked me if she could preach in church the way she already "preached" in Sunday school. When I would ask my daughter what she wanted to address the church about, she would give long lists of prayers, statements about God, various death announcements, and calls to action. She reflected our congregation nicely.

But because the minister's daughter was not my idea of an appropriate guest preacher (it's a well-known fact that she was after my job), I would send her back to Courtney with these requests, and somehow, perhaps in prayer circle time, she was finding her opportunity to give testimony. I sensed that Courtney would have the gifts and abilities to introduce this idea to the children, and I thought it ought to come through her and the volunteers, rather than through me, because they were already trusted and admired by the children.

Still, when Courtney and I met the week after I shared my testimony, I noticed that Courtney was looking uneasy as our conversation continued. Her brow wrinkled, and I wondered if I had misread her natural enthusiasm for my project. "Is something wrong?" I asked.

"Well," she said quietly, "it occurs to me that if I'm going to ask the children to do these testimonies, I really need to lead by example."

"Do you mean you would give your own testimony to the children downstairs?" I asked, although I would have been shocked if she had said yes. For one thing, Courtney hated public speaking. She is the type of teacher who does not lecture from on high but instead gets right down on the floor with the children. Second, she is a private person, and while I myself had heard her refer to her strong faith, I had never heard anything close to a testimony. I wondered what she would tell the children, if indeed she was offering, which I hoped she was.

"No," she replied. "I don't want to do that." My heart sank in disappointment. "What I think I should do is give my testimony in church, like the other adults have done. Then the children will see their Christian education director doing the same thing upstairs that we'll be doing downstairs."

I was thrilled. I knew that Courtney did not relish the idea of doing this, but as a teacher, she wanted to lead by example. Now that I look back on it, all the adults who gave testimony in church were leading by example.

Courtney went on to give her beautiful testimony in worship. She shared a story in church about how she had been so positively affected by her time at Silver Lake Church Camp, a United Church of Christ facility that children of our church still attend. The children were there for her testimony, as they usually were, since we made a point of putting testimonies in the first section of the service, before children left for Sunday school. They got to hear how, at Silver Lake, Courtney had wondered if she was called to the ministry. Now she was a teacher in the public schools and our Christian education director. The children were learning, in her testimony, about the complexities of call and vocation.

Courtney continued the conversations downstairs on Sunday, inviting the children to give their testimonies during their circle time. Together, they were sharing their experiences of God, not upstairs in church in front of everyone, but in their own gathering time as children.

What we did have upstairs in church were teen testimonies, specifically from the confirmands. Sam, our associate minister, introduced the practice that on the eve of confirmation, the youth would spend the night at a beautiful retreat center on Long Island Sound. There, they would finalize faith statements they had been considering all year in confirmation class. The next Sunday, before being confirmed, the youth would stand at the lectern, the same place where adults gave testimony, and give their own words. This practice has come to be a highlight of the confirmation process, and I have no doubt that the youth's willingness to do this was directly related to having seen adults do it too. Many of these young confirmands' own parents had given testimony.

Each year, the confirmands seemed to grow more comfortable speaking about their faith, as the practice of testimony had become more accepted in our church. Sometimes the confirmands projected their views about how the world should be cared for and improved, sometimes they were humorous, sometimes they became tearful when describing the important event they were about to embark on. We certainly had been tearful, as the listeners.

The confirmands' testimonies were much more theological than the adults'. Having spent a year receiving instruction on United Church of Christ polity and theology, they often referred as part of their testimony to their own baptism, something I have never heard an adult do. They more freely referred to Jesus and their own call from God. Perhaps this is the freedom of youth—or the effects of the last night of sleep deprivation at the retreat center. I actually believe it reflected the careful teaching they received through the confirmation curriculum, but also the confidence they had that what they said would be cherished and honored by the church.

Testimonies for youth have now expanded to include the chance for them to testify after mission trips. These are wonderful testimonies that serve to thank the church for nurturing and sponsoring them in their mission, and they are less formal, since they are not attached to the confirmation ritual. When the youth offer testimony about their mission trip, the whole congregation gets to be involved in the trip, rather than just the small number who were physically present.

Still, in the area of children, youth, and testimony, there remains much work to be done. One possible next step could be to treat youth testimonies as adult testimonies and to intersperse them throughout the church year. Could children take their testimonies from Sunday school and share them with the whole congregation? What sort of teaching would need to take place to prepare them for that experience? There is still much that could be explored in how testimony can be a part of Christian education.

Even so, I know that in watching others give their testimony, our children and youth have grown in understanding about the life of faith and in their own confidence as well. In worship, children began to offer their own prayer requests and announcements, seeming to understand that if the adults can do this, they should as well. They clearly are capable of sharing in worship in more ways than just reading Scripture.

I should note that in that first part of worship, when the children are present, they often rustle around and make the normal noises of active children confined to hard church pews. On certain Sundays, when they do stay in church for my sermon, I compete with a certain amount of noise. But during testimonies, I notice that the children are quite still and silent. They appear to find these moments as fascinating as the adults do. Perhaps they can imagine themselves up there one day, sharing their faith.

At least for these children, this practice will be familiar to them. While their parents tentatively venture into the practice of testimony, reclaiming a rich Christian tradition that we had let go, their children are seeing it as the natural course of things. Imagine—a Congregational church where the children are raised with the expectation that they can share their Christian faith stories with one another freely. Even in New England? Stranger things have happened.

CHAPTER 9

Speaking of Grief

In testimonies, people spoke of life, but they also spoke of death and often referred to those they had lost. Some of our most effective testimonies included reflections upon a beloved grandfather and the lessons of faith learned at the knee of one long since passed. Testimonies, it turns out, are opportunities to thank not just the living, but the dead as well.

The word *testimony* here reminds me of the testimonial in which one person offers verbal tribute to another. Although there may be elements of testimonial tribute within a testimony, a testimony is more than a testimonial. A testimony points us back to God. So in thanking a beloved grandfather, the testimony goes on to thank God for the gift of life or for lessons learned.

Funerals can be times for offering beautiful testimonials, or testimonies, but these two are different. A loving eulogy may tell us a great deal about the deceased but very little about the God who gives us life. A testimony, on the other hand, points us from the life, to the loss, to the redeeming grace of God who heals, and may also reflect upon the life of a particular person. It is thrilling for the congregation when testimony breaks through testimonials at a funeral, as thrilling as realizing, as a child, that you have graduated from paddling in the wading pool to swimming all the way across the pool. A testimony goes deeper into grief than any personal tribute can, for it brings with it the experience, presence, and promise of God.

In her chapter "Dying Well" from the book *Practicing Our Faith: A Way of Life for a Searching People,* seminary professor Amy Plantinga Pauw writes about how the church responds to the inevitability of death.

> This answer is not merely a matter of interior, personal conviction. It takes concrete form through the patterned life of the Christian community, molding the way we live and the way we die. In the weekly rhythm of the Christian life, the community gathers to celebrate the resurrection, God's final victory over death. Every year during the season of Lent, it focuses on Christ's death on the cross. And in other rhythms, too, the church surrounds those enduring the pain, fear and grief of death with visible, tangible signs of assurance and hope. Through impromptu conversations and well-planned funerals, through singing, prayer, and anointing with oil, through gifts of flowers and food, the Christian community acts out its beliefs.[1]

To Pauw's list of practices that bring about comfort and convey hope, I would now add the practice of testimony. One testimony at our church played such a role not just for the grieving but for the whole church, and for one woman in particular. Here, after the practice of testimony on Sunday mornings had been with our church for a couple of years, a grieving woman used the practice in order to finish what had been left unfinished and by doing so allowed the wider community to act out its beliefs.

Julie was a long-term member of the church, having grown up and raised her now grown daughter in the same Sunday school. She had served on many committees, from Christian education to her current position as a deacon, where she was entrusted with the spiritual and worship life of the church. Julie was the primary caregiver for her mother, who had also been an active and appreciated church member but had in recent years been confined by dementia to the healthcare unit of a retirement community. While Julie was able to provide the best of care for her mother, the stress of visiting and contending with the painful realities of this disease must have worn on Julie, as they would on any devoted daughter. When her mother died, she was exhausted, and when she attempted to gather her siblings for a funeral service, she found that their own illnesses prevented them from coming to Connecticut at that time.

So Julie invited me to preside over a tiny graveside committal service and determined that she would postpone the memorial service. At the time of the graveside service, I worried as her pastor that the memorial service would either never take place or, in its postponement, become an added source of stress, since this often happens to families who postpone. But of course, I respected and understood Julie's decision. Since her mother had died at a late age, there would not be many local mourners, so without the siblings, a service did not make sense.

Months went by and Julie struggled with her brothers' schedules and poor health, and it did appear that the service would never take place. In addition, Julie fell into a serious sadness that lasted many months but from which she eventually recovered. As Julie emerged from her melancholy and once again became involved in her communities, including the church, she realized that by not completing the rituals around her mother's death, by not being able to hold the memorial service, she may have added to her own stress and loss. Yet without her siblings, the problem of who could attend such a service remained.

Finally, Julie approached me and asked if, on an early January Sunday, she could prepare and offer her own testimony. She wanted to speak about her mother, about the church, and about the grace she had experienced in her own healing from depression. She wondered if Epiphany Sunday would be most appropriate, because this is the day in the Christian liturgical calendar when the wise men realized they were meeting the Savior in the baby Jesus. It was and is a day of remarkable realizations. Julie wanted to share her own epiphanies around loss and grieving.

As we planned for the day, Julie asked if Margaret, another member of the church, could offer words as well. Margaret is a loving, wise, and respected elder of our church who had shared a friendship with Julie's mother. Could she speak on Epiphany Sunday as well? By now, Julie was receiving word from friends and neighbors who had heard what she was doing that they wanted to attend our church that Sunday out of respect for Julie but also out of curiosity about the church that was putting all this together. We began to worry that the service of corporate worship was going to turn into a funeral service for one individual, so Julie and I agreed that her words about her mother would be just one piece of the service but not its entire focus. Still, she received more news that friends, and now, ironically, one of her brothers, would be attending as well.

Julie offered to host a special reception after the service in our formal upstairs parlor for her guests and the entire church.

At this point it was really starting to feel like a funeral that happened to be on Sunday morning, so we discussed again that this service had to make sense to a stranger walking in our doors for the first time. I realized that my sermon would play a key role in whether or not any of this worked. And on top of it all, since it was Epiphany Sunday, somehow I would have to fit in those three kings.

Just when I thought we couldn't fit another thing in, Julie shared with me that one source of her own epiphany was the deep friendship she and her husband share with a rabbi in town. The rabbi, Jim, had offered not only his friendship but spiritual counsel as well. He had shared with Julie many of the Jewish practices and beliefs about mourning. Julie, in looking back over a year when she had not been able to hold a memorial service, was particularly struck by the Jewish admonishment to hold services shortly after the time of death, with the understanding that mourning lasts a year. As we spoke, she wondered if we might invite Rabbi Jim to come and offer his testimony during the service as well.

By now, I think I was developing a sense of openness about the whole thing as well as excitement about this unusual service, having two members and a rabbi offering testimony on a single day. You see, in introducing testimony to our church, I had definitely opened the door for more lay participation in worship. With that came the sense that laypeople could offer testimonies and other elements to worship.

I wonder if this would have occurred before the practice of testimony, but by that time, I had been approached by many people about adding all sorts of things in worship. You really cannot invite people to share their stories of faith in front of hundreds of people and then be surprised when they want to introduce other things into worship as well. For this reason, it occurs to me that testimony is not a practice for the controlling pastor to introduce. Eugene Peterson writes eloquently about why a pastor ought to make herself "unnecessary," not to become useless, but to get out of the way and allow the laypeople to minister. Testimony requires a pastor willing to be unnecessary. If you can trust the Holy Spirit in one area, you must be open to its presence in other unexpected areas, which is a long way of saying that we invited the rabbi to give his testimony, too.

As it turns out, it was the Holy Spirit who ended up stirring all of these elements together into a very nontraditional Epiphany Sunday that brought in many epiphanies in its wake. Julie, in her words, spoke of more than her mother and brought forth a beautiful ecclesiology that explained all that God and the church had meant to her. Margaret was able to speak to the power and grace of an elder whom many of us had never known before her dementia set in. And the rabbi was the highlight of the service, reflecting on God and the practices of his religion as well his Jewish understanding of the afterlife, drawing us together in interfaith testimony. My sermon stressed the various epiphanies and attempted to cast a wide net over it all. What was remarkable was how many different things emerged from the service with three unusual testimonies around grief and one rather scattered sermon.

First, our attendance was greatly increased that day. It turns out that among Julie's local friends there were plenty of people who wanted to honor her mother's life, even if they had not known her personally. But would this same group have attended an ordinary memorial service? Many of them would have, but I believe that a number came out of curiosity about Julie's church. As she had told her friends about what we were planning, they had wondered at a church that would "allow" this. At the reception following the service, so many of Julie's friends commented on what a remarkable faith community we were that we could minister so intimately to one another and be so flexible.

The rabbi was particularly complimentary, understanding the preaching challenges such a service posed. He also expressed delight at being able to participate in an Epiphany Sunday service. He was familiar with interfaith worship, or exchanges between faith communities, and had preached at Christian churches before. But he was fascinated to be just one part of such a traditionally Christian Sunday morning service, with the focus on the three kings and the Christ child and our own practices, rather than on interfaith dialogue. We, in turn, appreciated his words, his wisdom, and his open spirit.

The interfaith exchange was a remarkable byproduct of our own Christian practice of hospitality. To me, this Sunday service was much richer than interfaith exchange for its own sake. Here, we were gathered in our own practices. Even though we believed differently, through our relationships we came together.

Within the congregation, people commented that the service seemed unusual with all the speakers, a sermon from me, as well as remarks from a rabbi. As worship leader, I did my best to explain and interpret the service for newcomers, but I am sure some remained baffled. Still, after so many positive comments from visitors, I was gratified. Without the practice of testimony, we would never have entered into such a service, and interestingly, it has not been repeated since. But as I mentioned earlier, testimony does open the door for suggestions of how to expand worship.

Many people were blessed that day with insights into their own grief, or perhaps prepared for a future grief, or soothed from a past grief. I realized later that when people said they appreciated the service, they meant something deeper. As Julie dealt with grief through her testimony, she ministered to others who grieve and have grieved. The subjects of death and loss became more a part of our community discussions, and I found myself in my preaching paying more attention to these themes after that Epiphany experience.

While we could not duplicate that particular Epiphany if we tried, we did come to understand as a church that grieving rituals can be as unique as the individuals and communities who grieve. And in giving people permission to give testimonies, you open the door to words and worship you might not expect but by which you may well be transformed. In testimony, we were reminded that the love of a community is indeed stronger than death.

But perhaps more important than the theme of grief was the fact that we opened ourselves up to a different way of planning church. As a pastor, that was the most initiative I had ever seen a layperson take in terms of requesting and then being a part of a particular Sunday morning service. It was through testimony that the laypeople of our church came to see that service as theirs to shape, and not just the property of the pastors. When a layperson approached me with her idea of testimony as a way through her grief, I learned something, as a pastor, about letting go.

CHAPTER 10

Building Stronger Leaders

Eugene Peterson, a pastor who writes for pastors, is critical of the way many ministers spend their time. In his books, he draws out similar critiques of what the ministry has become. He argues that pastors ought to spend more time on the work of spiritual leadership, on prayer, preaching, and relationships, and less time on what he sees as secular intrusions into the ministerial calling, or the "business" of the church.

Peterson came to this point of view after going to his church's board intending to resign. When they talked together about why he was resigning, he came to realize that he was spending a great deal of time on things he felt were not central to his calling. As he tells the story, his board challenged him to organize his work as he saw fit and leave the committee meetings and the running of the church to them. Out of this rather unusual experience, he has written about a model for ordained ministry that pastors recognize as extreme but intriguing. As he calls pastors to attend to the spiritual well-being of their churches and to resist the worldly temptation to obsess about numbers and growth, he also argues that ordained ministers should have more respect for the ministry of the laity and empower them to do many of the things that some pastors do poorly. He makes this argument in the hope that by digging in and doing what they are trained to do, pastors will foster congregations with more spiritual depth. He suggests that pastors who do this will be more likely to sustain longer ministries in one setting. He wants to break the current pattern of pastors moving from one church to another like anyone else on a career ladder, sacrificing depth in one parish for newness and change.

In one well-known example, Peterson argues that pastors should be "unnecessary," as he explains in *The Unnecessary Pastor: Rediscovering the Call.*

> I don't mean worthless or irrelevant or shiftless. I mean unnecessary in three ways in which we are often assumed to be necessary:
>
> 1. We are unnecessary to what the *culture* presumes is important: as paragon of goodness and niceness. . . .
> 2. We are also unnecessary to what *we ourselves* feel is essential: as the linchpin holding a congregation together. . . . We have important work to do, but if we don't do it, God can always find someone else—and probably not a pastor. . . .
> 3. And we are unnecessary to what congregations insist that we must do and be: as experts who help them stay ahead of the competition.

Peterson goes on to comment:

> I am in conversation right now with a dozen or so men and women who are prepared to be pastors and who are waiting to be called by a congregation. And I am having the depressing experience of reading congregational descriptions of what these churches want in a pastor. With hardly an

exception they don't want pastors at all—they want managers of their religious company. They want a pastor they can follow so they won't have to bother with following Jesus anymore.[1]

I would never use such words to describe the members of the church I serve, but I understand Peterson's critique of many churches, for I have seen some that operate like religious companies rather than communities of faith. But I include Peterson's comment, because I believe that practices such as testimony, the sharing of our faith story, draw us closer to a Christ-centered community of faith. If we are tempted to operate as a religious company interested only in its own membership numbers or financial health (which I hope we would never be!), all it would take is one testimony to remind us what we are really here for. In testimonies it is the small stories that would probably not make much of an action movie that touch us the most. The words from a member about how the church and her faith lifted her up after the loss of her mother, the story of how a couple journeyed from church to church before feeling that God had brought them "home," the revelation that some sit in pews filled with doubt but feel the presence of God through the kindness of other human beings—these are the small stories that remind us that what God has in mind for pastors and congregations is greater than any career ladder or publicity plan. Something deeper is going on.

I also refer to Peterson because I believe that our congregation had a strong sense of themselves as ministers and Christian leaders and that they do indeed follow Jesus, but that testimony has strengthened that conviction. I am convinced that strong lay leadership will be bolstered by the practice of testimony, and where lay leadership is weak, it might also be

fostered. You cannot invite people to tell their faith stories to
one another and then be surprised when they become spiritual leaders of the church, and then, spiritual leaders to one
another. Once they have testified in church, they will naturally come forward with ideas about other aspects of church
life. For a congregation, this is a great blessing.

Some churches tend to have strong lay leadership, and there
is generally not a sense that the pastor automatically trumps
everyone else. Even though the pastor and the pastor's office
are both held in respect, the pastor is still one member of the
church with one vote at the annual meeting and must earn
any influence she hopes to have. But with numerous committees and growing numbers of activities, we have many slots to
fill each year. We fill them, but this is one area where we might
be tempted to act like the religious company Peterson looks
down upon. Rather than calling disciples, we slip into filling
slots on a nominating report just to get it done. Sometimes, as
busy as we are with good things, we can slip into the busyness
of the world leading up to Christmas and view the godly work
of the fall nomination of new leaders as just another job. So
what you will read below is how we struggled with this in the
fall of 2003 and how testimony helped us recover our sense of
calling at what is often a stressful time in churches: nominating season.

Where Are the New Leaders?

We gathered around the table at the church council meeting
aware that we had a few gaps in our leadership team. The
church council is the governing body of the church, made up
of the chairs of the major committees and officers of the church.
Our church membership was very transitional. In our con-

text, a college town with a recessional economy, people tend to move in and out fairly fluidly. The board chairs were reporting that after the departure of a number of key leaders to the greener pastures of wealthy Fairfield County or jobs further away, we had a few vacant slots on a number of committees. The nominating committee would have to fill not only the usual number of slots this year, but some extras.

As key leaders of the church, council members tend to put in the most hours at meetings, and sometimes they worry that no one else will want to make that commitment. Every church has this core group of people who give the most of themselves to the church. Even as they testify at meetings about how much serving the church means to them, sometimes I notice that when they approach others to serve, they do so not out of a sense of joy, but apologetically.

"The meetings aren't all that long, except in the fall when we do the budgets. Sure, you could skip every other one if that helps."

Or, "You've already served on the three other major boards. Haven't you wanted to be a deacon too? We need to fill the slot."

Or, "I'm stepping down from this job feeling exhausted. Now, it's your turn." Ouch.

Or, worst of all, "The hours are short, the work easy, and the commitment minimal . . . so naturally we thought of you!"

As we considered our leadership shortage, I worried that our busyness as a church would lead us into a discussion about who we could press into service, rather than who God was calling. But this fall at council, the board came up with a much more creative idea. As they discussed how much they really enjoyed serving in their own positions, someone said, "Why don't we stand up in worship and tell people about the committees and what they do?"

At first I balked, since I've heard other churches do this sort of thing and it bores people to death—lengthy discussions of deacon's duties or intimidating lists of the heroic tasks of running the Christian education program. But after two years of including testimony in worship, the church leaders were thinking differently about how they used the worship time to convey information about the life of the church. We had had many discussions about our desire that we make "no Godless announcements," and by now testimony was a part of how we were thinking. So one leader said, "Let's make them testimonies. Let's talk in worship about how we have experienced God in our lives through serving on these committees."

That suggestion showed me how the practice of testimony was shaping us for the better. For years we had all had wanted the nominating process to be more about calling and vocation and less about "filling slots." I knew that we had been moving closer to that every year, as our committee meetings themselves had become places of testimony, where people felt fed in the Spirit by coming to these meetings. But in committees where the familiar business model reigned and attention was not paid to members' relationships with God and one another, attendance fell off.

As more committees focused on building relationships with one another, with the experience of God as the context, we were losing fewer people to boredom, but still, we had those leadership slots to fill as people moved away. As the leaders at the church council that night discussed the idea of offering their testimonies about their experiences as leaders, they grew less concerned about those slots and more excited about who from each committee would speak. Several chairs volunteered on the spot, while other chairs became excited about who they might recruit.

The council decided to offer the testimonies without mentioning the need to recruit during the fall. They decided to speak in the spirit of the other testimonies, offered without agenda. They understood the testimonies as opportunities to share about the life of faith. But when the worship bulletins were printed, we called them "Leadership Testimonies." These testimonies would still be personal stories about God, but the theme would be leadership in the church. In this way, they were like the "giving testimonies." They were testimonies with a theme, which is to say that unlike the Lenten testimonies, they could not be "about anything you want as long as it is not Godless." We did remind one another at that council meeting to include God in the leadership testimonies, but by now that was more of a running joke than a real concern.

These testimonies were also similar to our giving testimonies in that they marked a new way of viewing a subject. Just as early giving moments were about the church's need for money but later evolved into testimonies about our need to give, these leadership testimonies were going to focus less on the church's need for new committee members and more on the joy of service from those who had experienced it first-hand.

The first leadership testimony came from a deacon, for deacons are the spiritual leaders of the church, concerned with worship and our community life. We felt they ought to lead this effort within worship. However, it was not the senior deacon who had attended the council meeting, but a woman who was one of what we jokingly call "deacon on deck," meaning she was preparing to serve as senior deacon two years hence. Grace immediately volunteered herself, and I could see why. She consistently spoke about her joy in being a deacon. Her words always reminded the group why their work mattered.

A leader with a certain personal elegance, Grace brought new style to church social functions (for example, our Silver Teas) and had a strong sense of the importance of the deacon's practice of hospitality.

In her testimony, Grace spoke about how she had never expected to be a church deacon. In taking us through her surprise, Grace, a professional, well-spoken woman, anchored her testimony with a story about, of all things, Barbie dolls! As she considered all the roles she had played as a girl with her Barbies, she told us that she had never played "church." I saw, as Grace whimsically wove together Barbies and her Christian walk, the remarkable uniqueness of testimonies, which in turn showed the congregation the many models of lay leadership in our church.

People loved Grace's testimony on so many levels. First, any testimony involving a discussion of a Catholic-Protestant upbringing would be a big hit, as was any testimony about being raised by parents who did not come from the same religion. Grace described a childhood familiar to many, with one Protestant parent and one Catholic, and why in the end, she had found her adult church home at Redeemer.

But most interesting to me in her testimony was her use of the Barbie doll as an example. In describing her surprise at being a church deacon, she remembered that she had never played "church" with her Barbies. First, this part of her testimony opened up a church-wide conversation about Barbie dolls, which was as animated as any I had ever seen. Some women confessed to still having their Barbies, with all their little shoes and outfits preserved. Other women talked about hating Barbies, from their tiny waists to their permanently disfigured high-heeled bare feet. The men listened with interest to the passion we women brought to the subject of those little 12-inch dolls. Yet, Grace's use of the dolls was inspired, because for many children, dolls are the windows into vocation. As girls, we literally tried on roles when the dolls changed clothes. I was reminded that at a church auction we held, one of the most popular items was a set of doll clothes hand made for the popular "American Girl" doll series. A church member had sewn a little black clergy robe with hand-embroidered stoles in every liturgical color. When that item came up for auction and people "Oohed" and "Aahed," it hit me how much church members longed to see their liturgical life, or their faith life, represented in doll culture, as if they knew, in a strange reversal, that doll clothes might make it *real*.

So when Grace told us about all the roles she played with Barbies but how church roles were absent, she was also saying something about women's culture (for church leadership was not a fantasy that girls in her childhood world entertained) and about the secular world's denial of the sacred. (You can buy a Barbie camper, a Barbie dream house, a Barbie plane, and a Barbie horse, but I've never seen a Barbie church.) It was an insightful and playful testimony that sent us out with much to think about. Or at least wanting to go home and get out that old Barbie camper and all those little plastic shoes from the attic.

Piano Keys

Rick's testimony for the music committee stretched our definitions of testimony in a different way. It was offered spontaneously, with Rick seated in front of a microphone at the sanctuary's grand piano. He spoke while he trailed his fingers up and down the keyboard, almost in the style of a lounge singer.

Rick is a composer of jazz and rock piano as well as synthesizer music who has played for us in worship on many occasions, and seeing him at the piano made sense. I thought it was a wonderful example of how, like Grace, he could bring in an object, here quite audibly, a piano, in order to make his points. I was struck that in testimonies, people used their unique gifts. I thought it was wonderful that Rick, a musician who loves to improvise, was able to make that a part of his testimony, so that the words and the musical chords wove around one another.

On later Sundays, when he simply played in worship, I found myself recalling his words and the role he played in the church. I began to consider that musical expression in worship was another form of testimony.

Pluripotential Cells

Another example of a testimony about leadership in the church that brought out the unique interests of the speaker was Jonathan's testimony about his service on the Christian education committee. Jonathan is in the medical field and in the past was a science teacher, so it only made sense that when it came time for him to give a testimony, he brought in a little of the science lab, a little of the hospital, and even a little joke about his own balding head.

Jonathan

My name is Jonathan, and I am a member of the Christian education committee and an assistant with the youth groups. So you're probably wondering what an almost-40-year-old guy with no kids is doing involved with youth concerns.

Of course, I realize this begs the commentary, "Maybe, in some ways, he just hasn't grown up?" If truth be told, I know there are certain moments when my fiancée might agree with that, however infrequent they may be, and come to think of it, in recent years, I have reverted to my "hair style of infancy."

More seriously and simply, I'm involved with youth because they are God's gift for tomorrow. I grew up in a family of seven kids. I've got 20 nephews and nieces. I've been a teacher, a coach, a counselor, and now a caregiver to children, and it has been these life experiences that have convinced me that children are the most meaningful investment we have toward a more peaceful, more just, and more loving world. That's why I'm here, to share this belief, which I hope strikes a chord and stirs a similar conviction with you. See if this fits.

Recently, the popular press has given much attention to the stem cell. Stem cells are unique in that they differentiate and develop into all of the various cell types that make up our bodies. They have the potential to become anything! For this reason, they are often referred to as pluripotential cells. Influenced by all that surrounds them throughout embryonic development, they can become anything from among the 60 trillion cells of our body. In the same way, I look at children as pluripotent lambs of God, and as members of their surrounding community we uniquely influence and shape their development as wards of the future. Every child is then a marvel of pluripotency—each with their own unique set of raw materials having the capacity for wonderful possibilities when they are influenced by the love of God that surrounds them during their most formative years.

Consider for a moment just one element of this pluripotency: children's curiosity that manifests itself in the form of seemingly endless streams of questions. They want answers! Oh, they start off with the easy questions, but it isn't too long before they catch us so off-guard that we squirm and dodge to try to change the subject. How does a fly walk upside down? What is lightning and thunder? How do we remember? Try to pull answers to some of those out of your hat!

And, as they explore God's presence in their lives, the curiosity deepens. What is faith? Where does faith come from? These are tough, important, and vital questions that mark pivotal moments when a child listens and learns.

In my life, I appreciated most the adults in both academic and faith communities who took the time to acknowledge my curiosity and answer my questions. In this faith community as well, it is you and me, the adults, who introduce and model the love of God to the children. We are responsible for assisting them and helping them understand God's way in their world and God's involvement with them. We are responsible for supporting and perpetuating our children's beliefs in God's promises, not just with simple answers to their questions, but also by providing:

1. Youth-oriented activities centered around the church year
2. Structured, age-appropriate curricula taught by their adult mentors working in teams (Some of whom, by the way, are still needed! Courtney would be happy to speak with you at the Silver Tea about how to join our teams of teachers!)

Additionally, we aim to nurture a faith in our youth that reflects Redeemer's worship and mission goals by encouraging involvement:

3. In worship services and other church-sponsored events
4. In Christian missions in the New Haven community

God calls us, and, in turn, our children—through us— with the invitation: "Come to me. Your faith has made you well. I will give you rest for your soul . . . and direction in your life."

Could I have all the children stand? This is our investment. And now, the Christian education committee—please
stand. The Christian education committee is a special opportunity to be involved in introducing children to the love of God
that passes all our understanding and to help launch and
sustain their relationships with God to last a lifetime and into
eternity.

I should note that after church that Sunday, the Christian
education committee recruited all the teachers it needed, not
by pressure or guilt, but by showing the church the joy that
one man felt in his ministry with the children. It was a great
day for the children as well, who really enjoyed seeing someone who worked with them talk about why he did it.

So often we in the church have a rather paltry view of lay
ministry. Even when we speak of valuing lay leadership, we
can leave the church members feeling that while they are good
enough to make decisions about coffee hour or the budget,
the real work of ministry belongs to the ministers. We limit
the term *lay ministry* by using it only to describe the ways
laypeople do the work of ministry in the local church, from
serving on committees to ushering to managing endowments.
But a wider vision of lay ministry recognizes that they minister when they are out in the world, exemplifying their faith,
doing what God has called them to do, wherever God has
called them to do it. Lay ministry is about making one's faith
a way of life.

In the testimonies of these lay leaders, their lives were the
pallet from which they colored in their stories about God. For
Grace, her own childhood and the whimsical Barbie theme
opened up new ways of thinking about vocation for the rest
of us. For Rick as a musician, it was notes of music that drew

us in, so the person he was in his day-to-day life came shining through in his testimony. And only Jonathan, with his background in science, medicine, and children could have brought us the beautiful and extraordinary phrase: "I look at children as pluripotent lambs of God."

When these and others spoke about their leadership in the church, it was clear that God was using them in a rich ministry, unique as they were. The testimonies of leaders in the church reminded us that while we may all be created in the image of God, what a vast image that must be—to produce such a mix of gifts, talents, and callings.

I imagine that those listening thought about their own quirky gifts and came to imagine where they too could contribute. Their vocation was encouraged, I hope, and their curiosity piqued. How might their ideas and interests come into play in the church's ministry? Testimonies of leaders open us up to consider our own callings in new ways. Many people told me after these testimonies that they had never considered serving in a particular way until the words they heard one Sunday opened them up to a new sense of themselves and what they could offer. From Barbies, to piano keys, to pluripotential cells, our imaginations were opened up to see that in God's house there must be a place for everyone.

Jonathan described the uniqueness of calling so well that day: "Each child is then a marvel of pluripotency, each, with his or her own unique set of raw materials having the capacity for wonderful possibilities when they are influenced by the love of God that surrounds them during their most formative years." Testimonies like that one strengthened the lay leadership in the church, as more people started to wonder what God was calling them, in their uniqueness, to do.

CHAPTER 11

Listening to Testimonies

As we grew in our practice of testimony, I was able to speak to the people who gave the testimonies as well as to those who heard them and to make notes on their reactions. In addition, three formally gathered groups in particular—the deacons, the financial development committee, and the women's book group—offered feedback. Two of those groups, the deacons and the financial development committee, actually planned testimonies as part of their work, inviting people to speak. So it was only natural that at their meetings they would evaluate what we were doing. I also sought feedback as we went along from other committees, from my pastoral relations team, and from individuals who over the years had told me how much someone's words touched them. In considering how people heard testimonies, I also gained some insight into how to plan them.

Financial Development Committee

In some ways, the testimony effort began with this group, although as testimonies began, they were called "giving moments." This committee was responsible for encouraging pledging in the church, so they were the group who first asked people to stand up on Sunday morning and speak about giving. Unlike other events at other churches that may sound similar, this testimony was not to be a simple pitch for money but was set out explicitly as an opportunity to reflect on God. Because members talked about their experience of God, I consider these to be our first testimonies. As our congregation expanded the practice of testimonies beyond the pledging season and opened them up to all subjects, the "giving moments" came to be called "giving testimonies" by the next year.

So this committee, even as members rotated on and off, understood the power of testimony. They took their role in selecting people very seriously, and always gave thought to striking the right balance among the speakers, so that a 25-year-old may be in a good position to explain giving to other impoverished graduate students, and a long-term member may be able to speak more directly to those who had experienced more time with the church.

But what we discovered was that quite often, people most liked the testimonies of people different than themselves. Perhaps these testimonies offered more surprises to the listener. Often a younger member would say it was a long-term member speaking about how our church building came to be built who convinced her about giving toward the church budget. And older members would often express enthusiasm for younger speakers, hearing in their words fresh insights into the life of the congregation.

As the pledging season progressed, and we waited to see what people would commit to pledge to the church financially for the year ahead, it became the custom for the committee to reflect on how the testimonies were going through group conversation and reflection. I was always impressed that they did not evaluate the testimonies cynically or, heaven forbid, numerically and financially. The committee would reflect on whether or not they felt the speaker had been "spiritual enough" and worried when there was too much talk about paint, roofs, and dollars. Sometimes they were disappointed when a testimony did not turn out to be a testimony, in other words, when the speaker spoke eloquently but neglected to mention God, Jesus, and the Holy Spirit. We always had to remind people to talk about God. But most of all, the committee found much to celebrate in the testimonies, and they were always surprised at the fresh ways people approached the subject.

In one testimony, for example, a young woman named Jalean, with an engaging and cheerful demeanor, used the phrase "Hi!" as her refrain throughout, as she reflected on everything from the lack of women's leadership in the church she was raised in, to pledging, to her understanding of the church as a place where God says "Hi!" to us. After that, the word "Hi!" took on new meaning for us as a church, and we came to know her so much better. When I asked her how it felt to speak that day, she said it felt good to be known better. In a sense, her testimony had become the way she said "Hi" to the people in the church she didn't know.

Social connections were always sparking up as people listened to testimonies. The news that the speaker was from Minnesota would invariably draw together a little cluster of displaced Minnesotans talking about what life in New England was like. Testimonies, and the little details of life that they reveal, opened the door for new connections among the members. We were always discovering we had more in common than we thought, so listening to testimonies, and learning about one another, strengthened the relationships in the church.

The financial development committee came to assume that giving testimonies would be at the heart of the stewardship and pledging season. And I believe this practice shaped our church's attitude toward money, for we saw the giving campaign as about much more than money. Relationships trumped money, be it our relationships with one another within the body of Christ, or our relationship to Christ himself. Listening to testimonies can serve to build community and deepen our faith, and the giving testimonies became another form of treasure that we offered up to God.

The Deacons

The deacons, that board that is responsible for the community and spiritual life of the church, were the next group to consider testimonies, and they continued to lead as the speakers and as the recruiters of other speakers. We began with the season of Lent, and then moved to hearing testimonies at all different times. Sometimes the ministers and moderator would ask someone to testify, sometimes a volunteer would approach the minister, but mostly the deacons shepherded this process. As a result, at deacons' meetings, they often discussed the testimonies that had passed, even evaluating them, not so much as to "quality" but asking whether or not they had really been testimonies, had really spoken about the person's experience of God. The same group that was on the lookout declaring "No Godless announcements" was also in charge of reminding folks "No Godless testimonies either!"

Our deacons were the most relational board in the church. At their meetings, they spent most of the first hour sharing with one another in a process called "good and new," followed by prayer. "Good and new" is a time when we would go around the room inviting people to share some experience that has been either good or new. The "new" allows the possibility of sharing something sad, or hard, so that this time does not slip into a bragging session or a falsely happy time. People will share things they are understandably proud of, such as a child's success, a new job, or an experience in which they grew, but they will also share hard things, like a job loss, an illness, or a concern about the world.

This "good and new" ritual predates testimonies and was introduced by one of the deacons, but it was out of that experience that I think we began to consider what it would mean to allow people to share their own "good and new" in the context of worship, and in the light of God. When testimony became a practice, I felt the "good and new" ritual changed, as we tried to speak not just about our experiences in life but also about how we saw God at work in them. So the "good and new" deacons' ritual opened us to testimony, and then testimony opened the deacons to see that "good and new" did not have to be Godless. Listening to testimonies in church helped the deacons to share testimony with one another at their meetings. My hope was that this board's community experience could be spread throughout the church. The deacons moved us in that direction, and testimonies helped us get there.

Listening to testimonies builds community, often in surprising ways. Humor has played a vital role in making connections. One man used as his jumping-off point his ugly tie collection and wore a rare specimen that Sunday. With humor, he drew us right in for a serious testimony about the witness of faith he had received from his grandfather. But it all began with a silly tie.

At times, the themes of testimonies have been delightfully offbeat. I believe that in the oddness of themes, we send a message that church and theological reflection are for everyone, and that is not just one type of person in a given church. For some people, Barbies and odd ties open the door to something much deeper, and these two testifiers made that move with grace and wit.

The deacons, who recruited the testifiers, were also careful not to stick to long-term members or people who were already known to be eloquent. Sometimes, they discovered a talent for public speaking in someone we did not suspect would even agree to do it. Other times, the testimony given in the most halting style or softest voice offered the greatest blessing. The deacons, already relational, saw themselves as planting that seed to speak within the congregation. So as they listened, they continued to look around to find fresh voices in our church. The more they heard, the more they wanted to hear, and therefore keep the practice of testimony going.

The Women's Book Group

The other group I looked to for feedback in this project had nothing to do, as a group, with planning the testimonies, and so did not have an investment in how the practice was received. This third group, the women's book group, included mostly retired women, a few of whom could not regularly attend worship. So when we met twice a month, there was usually a time of about half an hour before we started discussing whatever book we were reading when we simply caught up on the "holy gossip" of the church, sharing in a loving way who was ill, who was moving, who showed up in church, and who had not come in a while. Inevitably, we spent a little time reviewing the past couple of Sundays for those who weren't there, and it was a chance for me to receive feedback on worship.

This group long predates my ministry and was full of important leaders in the church, many of whom had a much longer tenure than I did as minister. This is probably the most forthright and plainspoken group in the church—which is to say, when someone is unhappy with something in worship, this is where you will hear about it first. I appreciated this, but I was curious to see how the testimonies would be received by this group and also by this generation.

I think this group received testimony as a positive influence in the service, with a few exceptions. I heard occasionally in this group the complaint that worship services were too long. I might hear a comment like, "Last Sunday, we just had too many things going on in one service," or "Can't you schedule it so that there isn't a testimony and new members and communion all in one week?" In addition, I received complaints when the speaker did not use the sound system well or mumbled or could not be heard. But again, this was not really a complaint about testimony, but rather a desire to hear it better, which is, of course, understandable.

Many of the members of this book group gave testimonies themselves, and they reflected on deep and important aspects of our life together, sometimes teaching the rest of us about a history of the church we would not otherwise have known. One woman spoke about a time in the life of the church when women could not be deacons and explained that the "deaconesses," a group of women excluded from the male deacon duties of leading the church, were responsible for the duties associated with women's work. She told us she was the first woman asked to be a deacon (a real spiritual leader of the church) and how exciting that was.

Another member of this book group used time in her testimony to thank the two former pastors of the church, who encouraged her to go back to school and finish her college degree after her children were grown. The sharing of these stories then opened up great conversations in the book group and allowed newer members and older members to bond. So while this group throughout the years has offered some logistical feedback (services too long, speakers too quiet), they supported the content and the practice as a whole. Furthermore, they were moved spiritually by hearing one another's stories. For those raised in the church, it marked a change in that this was not a group accustomed to sharing faith and belief in the context of church. But they welcomed the candor of the speakers, and continued the conversations started in worship with one another at book group each meeting.

Negative Reactions to Hearing Testimony

Did everyone love the new practice of testimony? Of course not. I know that some rolled their eyes at the practice, but most of the negative feedback came in the form of constructive criticism. They did not dislike the practice so much as they wanted to tweak it to make it better. The criticisms helped us along the way as we grew into this new way of sharing our faith.

"I couldn't hear it."

The book group was not the only place where I heard logistical concerns. Other members of the church commented with displeasure when they could not hear a testimony. Here, I believe they were affirming the practice but simply wanting to be as fully engaged as possible in what the speaker was saying. They had every right to want to hear the testimonies, and I can understand their frustration when this was not possible.

However, this brings up an interesting dilemma about testimonies. Not everyone is a natural speaker. Not everyone who has something important to say is good at saying it. We realized this early on, as someone would begin to speak and a deacon or minister would reposition the microphone for the speaker, hoping to catch more of what he or she said. We worked with people who had not spoken in church before and coached them on how to use the microphone, but once they were up there staring out at all those people with a certain amount of stage fright, they would often forget what they learned.

Other speakers suffered from too much confidence. On a number of occasions the person giving the testimony, after agreeing to use the microphone, would, in the moment, decide to step away from the microphone saying something like, "I hate these things. Besides, nobody has trouble hearing my voice."

What they forget is that people with normal hearing may be able to follow them without the sound system. But our church has very poor acoustics for the spoken word, and when speakers stepped away from the microphone, their volume came through for people with hearing loss, but their words did not. Even worse, the hearing assistance devices the church provides actually work through the sound system, so a speaker who does not use the sound system suddenly changes volume for people with hearing aids and throws everything off.

Over and over again, we stressed the importance of using the sound system, and over and over again, in the spirit of the moment, people decided not to use it. The struggle is ongoing, and I have a few ideas why simply teaching and training don't work. I believe that some people have the perception that the microphone is somehow less intimate or perhaps signals some kind of inauthenticity or slickness. I also know that it can be frightening to hear your own voice booming back to you over the speakers, and this may be why people don't like it. Often people using a microphone will think they are too loud and will not realize that in the pews they sound just right. We also do not know what our own voice sounds like, because we hear it through our own "equipment." When we hear it through other channels, most of us think our voice sounds awful. So all this contributes to the microphone-trained speaker who suddenly, to my dismay, moves it aside and announces, "I don't need this thing!" only to exclude someone with that decision.

The fact is that if testimony is to work as a part of worship, it has to be heard by everyone, or it will rupture community rather than create it. So we continue to encourage people to use the sound system, even those who are just certain they "don't need it." We try to explain that while the speaker may not need it, many of our listeners do, and that it is only fair to include them in these special moments. We also must work to help people speak clearly and well, not out of a sense of performance, but as an issue of justice, so that in hearing, we might all be included in the same moment of grace.

"The service is too long."

One critique I heard about testimony in the congregation was that the services were getting too long. This was especially the case when we decided to have testimonies throughout a liturgical season, such as Lent or Advent, when the services already had many additional elements—from lighting the Advent wreath to longer musical selections to special liturgies. Sometimes people would complain there was just too much going on.

They would discuss the need to "schedule better," not really understanding the trickiness of church scheduling; for example, you may have planned a testimony months ago, but this baby needs to get baptized on a certain Sunday when her aunt is in town from the West Coast, and then a very special piece of music falls on the same day. My sense is that here, the critique was not about the testimony but about anything that resulted in the service being over 60 minutes long. Occasionally, the person who wanted a shorter service would point to "all the extras," which included testimony.

Longer services are the hazard of introducing a new practice into worship. (Or perhaps I should say that it is a hazard in those church communities with a low tolerance for God's grace after the sixtieth minute; we know who we are.) When worship is already planned for one hour, and then we add testimony, we could be adding three minutes or fifteen. In traditions that usually use testimony, such as the free-church and evangelical traditions, time is not as much of an issue, but for New England Congregationalists, it is a live one. Planning the many parts of worship, most of which depend on volunteers, means that by using testimony, we will occasionally get out later than some people would like, and these are the people who will then speak out.

I must admit that this type of criticism can be demoralizing for me as a minister, who feels that worship is the high point of my work and in my life. Furthermore, the people who enjoyed a service that lasted 75 minutes generally will not think to mention that they are *not* unhappy that worship lasted more than an hour. So the feedback you get is skewed toward the negative. I do make every effort to schedule testimonies in services that are not already full. When that doesn't work out as planned, I brace myself for a few comments.

In addition, the deacons worked to shorten parts of worship that could be shortened. We occasionally would fall into a pattern of lengthy announcements from the floor. In the same spirit of testimony, these personal announcements build community and foster relationships in a way that having the minister or one person make all the announcements does not. Yet, they can get out of hand, with people announcing things that will at best attract one person or that were adequately explained as printed announcements or could be communicated through phone calls or e-mails (for example, "The committee meeting is Thursday at 7:30 P.M.").

The practice of testimony actually gave the deacons an idea about how to deal with lengthy announcements. We decided that if testimonies could not be Godless, announcements should not be Godless either. Spurred on by the one limit we set on testimony, that it refer to God and be in some way theological, we applied the same standard to our announcements, and the senior deacon made an announcement and wrote a newsletter article to this effect. The deacons and other church leaders then agreed to model this in their own announcements by being both brief and theological. So instead of saying, "Please bring finger sandwiches to the Silver Tea," you could say, "In the spirit of Christian hospitality, please bring finger sandwiches . . ." or "As God calls us to be faithful stewards of our creation, please be aware of the church's recycling system at coffee hour."

I suspect that this requiring a theological rationale for an announcement resulted in some self-editing, as some people came to realize that if they couldn't think of a way to communicate an announcement theologically, it probably didn't belong in the worship service. And we continue to ask leaders to use the printed bulletin or e-mail and mail for logistical issues and meeting times, in order to allow worship to flow more quickly and smoothly.

So by adding testimony to worship, we also became aware of what we could cut out of worship and how to make that announcement period reflect the values of testimony and our church. Did this prevent long announcement periods in one fell swoop? Of course not. The deacons will probably revisit the issue and speak about it every year, but the conversations around the problem have been rich and meaningful. We have learned, for instance, that for now we value community and individual expression over efficiency (that is, we rejected the idea of eliminating announcements from the floor, although some members still think this is the best solution). We also learned that we did not value those announcements so much that they should be allowed to take over the worship services, and that sometimes limits and models can be provided that will enrich us all. I believe testimony helped us view this aspect of worship in a new way and helped us to see more deeply what we believe.

In the end, hearing testimonies strengthened our bonds as a community and gave us more enthusiasm for the practice. The more testimonies we heard, the more we wanted to hear. Furthermore, listening to testimonies shaped our worship, as we tweaked the service and the practice so that all might hear these words and be blessed by them. While hearing testimony added an element of chaos to worship in that it was unexpected and not in the control of the ministers, it mostly added excitement and more room for the Spirit to move. When we asked people what it felt like to hear testimonies, they responded with testimonies of their own—that their faith and community had been strengthened by the practice.

CHAPTER 12

The Testifiers Reflect

After we got used to hearing testimonies, I turned my attention to another question: What did it feel like to give a testimony? Usually I heard from people right after they had spoken in church, and they described things like nervousness, or their preparation process, or whether or not people laughed when the words were funny, or teared up as they heard a sad tale. These were immediate reactions from the speaker on the day of the testimony. But as the process deepened and I was able to interview the testifiers long after they had spoken, I began to learn that the people hearing the testimonies were not the only group being affected. The testifiers themselves were being transformed by the experience, not just in the moment, but also over time, mostly through the development of new relationships. They were sharing in worship and then forming new and transformed connections due to all the sharing and informal testimonies that took place at coffee hour, or in conversations much later. The testimony opened the door for people to approach the person who had spoken and share their own stories, which then changed the testifier.

A number of people enjoyed a real feeling of liberation. It was as if by giving their testimony, they threw aside a fear or a burden. I remembered David's first testimony, which had been about an earlier testimony at the church retreat in my living room where he described such a release:

> But when Lillian asked if people wanted to share their story, the spirit moved me to volunteer. I didn't know what would happen. There was a lump in my throat, my palms were sweaty. I took a leap of faith. It was a leap back from the wilderness into a new relationship with God, one based on my true nature. It didn't hurt that no one gasped or avoided me: in fact I felt affirmation. In moving me to speak from my heart, the spirit had also transformed my relationship with the congregation.
>
> I felt radiant, lighter than air. I felt that I had found home.
>
> I hope we can learn together how to call others from the wilderness to a home in this church.

I was struck by the dramatic way in which David described being transformed by testifying, of being made "radiant and lighter than air." That same phrase "radiant and lighter than air" was picked up by Ian, a deacon, in his reflections about how testimony had called him to see that radiance in others. Ian wrote of his experience just a few days after giving his testimony:

> After my testimony, I felt very peaceful. I put myself out there. Like at a rock concert, I was being carried overhead by the crowd. However, I have also had a few moments of fear. A public declaration of one's faith is a real commitment. No backsliding now! Whether it is related or not, I see people now more in terms of their faith, the *imago Dei,* and am beginning to understand the living God in Christ and our lives; and no longer am satisfied with and limited by the idea of God.

The words Ian used to talk about the experience—"beginning to understand," "no longer satisfied," and "after my testimony, I felt peaceful"—all pointed to an experience of being changed. He wasn't just saying the experience changed him. He described another force, "being carried," which sounds like the Holy Spirit. I believe that giving testimonies changes us not just through our own actions, but that in testifying we open ourselves up to being acted upon by God.

Julie, whose Epiphany testimony about losing her mother had been so important for the church, reflected a year after the testimony and two years after her mother's death about how much that testimony experience had meant to her and the healing she had felt: "There is no doubt that it was a really wonderful experience for me. I will put it into words for you. Since I have now passed (yesterday) the two-year mark, it will be good to think about it." Julie went on to comment on some people dear to her who were battling cancer and how hard illness and grief are, but as she noted that they might be near the end, she continued, "More the reason to give time and love to those around us and make the most of each day if we can." Julie's testimony had reminded her of what was important, even as she reflected on it a year later in a new time of grieving. I believe it was an experience that continued to uphold her.

Joe, the Roman Catholic who gave a testimony that ended with the words "I'm not even a Protestant," offered frank observations on how that testimony had changed his relationship to the church:

> Honestly, I thought about sharing a Giving Testimony for a
> long time. A few years ago, John called and asked if our
> family would like to do it. I said yes but then had to call and

back out once Lorraine said that she didn't want to. So, when Marilyn called me and asked me to do it, I asked if I could do it by myself just in case Lorraine said no again (she did). Being a "ham," I had no problem having the stage to myself.

The "I had already been thinking about doing it for a long time" theme came out many times among the people who testified. We never did receive more than a few volunteers to give testimonies, but those we asked often appeared to have been considering it for a while, perhaps waiting to be invited. Despite our calls for volunteers, there seems to be something honoring about being approached directly.

In addition to feeling honored having been asked, Joe saw his lay leadership affirmed after giving testimony, when he was asked and agreed to serve on the capital campaign committee, a large time commitment and key role in the church.

Joe went on to describe why he enjoyed giving the testimony and one of the reasons was that it gave him a chance to register disagreement with his pastor. As he remembered his testimony, he joked about "zinging" the minister with his reference to the fact that he does not always agree politically with the message coming from the pulpit. "I enjoyed writing my testimony. It brought back fond memories of my youth and of my time here at Redeemer. I was able to tell the church how much I have enjoyed my time here and zing you a little bit at the same time. I knew that you would take it well."

When I looked into American historical examples of testimonies, many of them had a polemical edge. Many of them, while being very much about God, were for or against various things in the world, from things that seem trivial to us, like card playing, to things that seem most important, like slavery. Similarly, in a number of testimonies the testifier would even speak against statements from the pulpit.

So I have come to see, in listening to other testimonies, the power of the preaching moment and that some of them long to give an alternative point of view. I know that people describe my preaching with words like "prophetic" when they agree with a political point I have touched on; or "annoying and partisan" when they don't. But the fact is that although I would never stand in the pulpit and tell people how to vote, my preaching probably leaves little doubt as to my own opinions on any given matter. I constantly bring in real world examples and often comment on pop culture—and I am not subtle in doing so.

When listening to testimonies, I learned that the laypeople enjoyed the opportunity to express another point of view. There was one run of testimonies in 2003 in which several speakers in a row made statements like these: "While I do not agree with everything our pastors say . . ." or "I come here not because I agree with what is preached all the time, but in order to be challenged" or "While Lillian and I may not agree on many issues. . . ." These were important moments for our church at the tail end of a year in which we had disagreed as a community about more than the usual number of issues. We had disagreed over issues of war and peace, the war with Iraq, the measures being taken to combat terrorism, gay marriage, and more locally we had been divided over a long strike by Yale employees. In all these situations, I had referred to the issues in preaching, or taken a clear public role that ended up in the press. So these moments of testimony, when church leaders could articulate their disagreement with me, however obliquely, served an important function in our church's life—to remind us that we were a community in which disagreement could be tolerated, even celebrated.

In one testimony, Marilyn, our moderator and the congregation's chief lay leader, said:

I love Church of the Redeemer. I love the sermons—and not only those that I can agree with. I love the sermons that force me to think about stuff from a perspective that I might not have considered. I love the sermons that tweak my conscience and complicate my thoughts.

During this particular run of testimonies, members' disagreements with me even became a source of mirth, as I begged, "Could someone please give a testimony in which they say they occasionally do agree with the pastor?" In some ways, my joking plea was an opportunity for me to model acceptance of other points of view and to convey my affection for those who disagreed with me, while not giving up my right to freedom of the pulpit. It also showed the church that the key lay leaders were not an insider's group who were in lockstep with the senior minister, but were in fact a diverse group chosen for their spiritual gifts rather than their politics. Marilyn had indicated that in her description of why she loved the church.

Marilyn later reflected on how the experience of giving testimonies had affected her. She referred to the Myers-Briggs Type Indicator, a subject she is an expert in through her work in corporate human resources. I remember Marilyn's testimonies with great fondness, so I was surprised that she recalled them with some insecurity:

> I've thought about my testimony experience and believe that one reason that I did not define my presentations as testimonies is that I don't believe I really revealed very much of myself in them. I was particularly moved by Amy's recently, and David's some time ago. They both seemed to really open up and allow us a glimpse of what was very close to their hearts. I don't think either of my testimonies was like that.

I am a very private person and only let people in under my own terms and in a very controlling way (very common for us INTJs). So, while both my testimonies did communicate what I wanted to communicate, they did not really get much below the surface of who I am and what my relationship to God means to me. Maybe, one day, I will (but I doubt it).

I have been very moved by the courage of those who have opened up and really shared their innermost feelings. I think it helps others in the congregation to hear and think, "I'm not the only one with these thoughts and feelings." But, I'm not there myself (yet?).

Marilyn's analysis of her testimony was interesting because I noticed something in it that I would notice in other recollections—a sense of comparison and self-criticism. It turned out that it was fairly common for people to compare their testimonies to others and to admire the ones most opposite from their own. I believe that just as many people were touched by Marilyn's words, even if they were more reserved, as by Amy's and David's, but Marilyn was harder on herself. I thought that Marilyn's testimonies played an important leadership function and tended to refer to the life of the church in concrete ways, which many people needed to hear. Yet the ones she most responded to were quite different from hers in that they were more personal and emotive. I saw as a pastor who heard them all, that just as the body of Christ has many members, Christ moves through all styles of testimonies. Sometimes the words we most need to hear are different from what we might say, but someone else can be blessed by our words as well. We need many styles of testimony, even if it does elicit comparison.

In addition, in her reflection, Marilyn raised an important point about her introverted personality type. Testimony is not going to be for everyone. Or at least, not everyone will be able to offer testimony in front of a large group of people in worship. Certain personality types are going to take to testimony easily, while others will struggle. Some people delight in self-revelation while others are shy and private and therefore will struggle more with the practice. Some of this came through when Courtney reflected on what it had been like to offer her testimony when she had been the director of Christian education:

> I thought about giving my testimony and the feeling that I had. I know that I was very nervous to make this speech not because standing up in front of the church and speaking makes me all that nervous, but that I would be letting the whole community into my private thoughts and feelings—things that I have only shared with my mom and maybe my dad.
>
> I recall stating that after attending Silver Lake the first year I felt more in touch with God than I had ever felt before that time in my life. I knew that I wanted to become a minister to serve God and do God's work. I remember that I lost that sense of God during my college years. I reflect back now and that was partly because my church no longer felt like a home and a community that I wanted to belong to any longer, which changed my sense of who I was.
>
> So to speak of this time of my life in front of the entire congregation really made me nervous. I think that just letting a group of people whom you don't completely know into your heart and mind and soul makes you just that much more vulnerable. That is scary. I don't easily let many people in.

Courtney's words were touching to me because she confirmed what I had suspected—that what we had asked her to do was difficult and did not come easily. The congregation would not have seen this because Courtney presented herself with grace and poise, but in her reflections I could hear how she had pushed herself. I also could hear that she was glad she had done it.

I felt sad when I listened to her description of coming back to her old church after that camp experience and then losing that sense of being called to ordained ministry. But I could rejoice with her that here in her new church, in this practice of testimony, she could share her faith and tell us about that call. She concluded her reflections with these words:

> Our church is one place that I let more people in than any-
> where else in my life. I do feel very comfortable there and that
> is why I could overcome my fear and anxiety of it all and
> testify my faith and belief in God to our church.

I am certain hearing others' testimonies added to that sense of safety and resulted in the gift that Courtney, a private person, gave to us that Sunday.

Many people commented with surprise at how people received their words. Some people were shocked at the response they got, including everything from spontaneous applause, to quiet, to tears. Joe remarked:

> I was ready for my testimony to be given in the midst of
> complete silence. The congregation can be a bit stodgy (as you
> know) and so you can imagine my joy when I was able to
> make people laugh. It made the experience that much more
> enjoyable. And when I was done, I was genuinely surprised at
> the warm applause that I received. I must say that it was a
> moment that I will always cherish (and, I have to admit, find
> myself replaying in my mind).

But he went on to describe the powerful emotions he was surprised to have evoked:

> After the service, many people approached me. Julie stands
> out because she was the first to come up to me. She told me
> how much she enjoyed my testimony and how I had made her
> cry. I told her that I didn't want people crying; I wanted them
> laughing. Nonetheless, as people came up to me at coffee hour,
> several of them stated that I had made them cry also. Perhaps I
> dwelt too long on some of the past, placed too much emphasis
> on what has gone wrong. My goal was not to depress people,
> but rather to let them know that certain things cannot be
> taken for granted and instead need to be fought for.

A number of people spoke to me after their testimonies about how the experience had changed them. So many of them were amazed by how many people came to speak to them afterwards and by all the connections they made as a result of their being brave enough to share their faith. Joe perceived a direct shift in his "standing" as a result of his testimony. He wrote of the experience:

> The one thing that stays with me about the entire experience is
> that my standing in the church seems to have changed. I've
> always thought of myself as one of the church's "characters"
> but now seem to be something else. Everybody seems to know
> me now (not always a good thing because I'm terrible at
> remembering names) and I can't imagine myself going some-
> where else to worship. That thought gives me both comfort
> and anxiety at the same time. Comfort because I have found a
> place that I love as much as any other church I have attended.

I do indeed miss St. Peter's, but having Church of the Redeemer in my life helps softens the blow.

As I reflect on all the words I heard from the testifiers, a few themes come through. They experience fear or anxiety, but that is replaced afterwards by a feeling of freedom or elation. Second, the testifiers realize that their testimony elicits other testimony in the conversations that follow. And third, by offering testimony, we offer ourselves in relationship to the community in a brand new way. New relationships will be formed, based on what people have heard you say.

Last, even though testifiers were delighted with the warm response they received, we are still human and cannot help but judge ourselves. We imagine that our words pale in comparison to those offered by another person, and even when testifying to God's grace, we still suffer under the need to do a good job. The Holy Spirit may be at work, but it does not take away everybody's anxiety all the time. It's still hard.

Human anxiety and insecurity are why we need to offer our testimonies to communities that will receive them with hospitality. It takes a lot of nerve to share our faith publicly and requires some people to stretch themselves almost to the limit. In hearing the reflections of those who had offered testimony, I was struck once again by the church's remarkable willingness to take that risk and struck also by how blessed a church may be by taking it. People I never expected to testify did, and developed relationships with God and one another that I could never have predicted. It is a practice that feels risky, but rewards richly.

CHAPTER 13

Speak the Vision

In our years with the practice of testimony, one of the most valuable things for me was hearing how people perceive their church. With testimony, you encourage members to reflect back to you their vision of the church, and in doing so, they reflect it to newcomers as well. We were constantly reflecting our ecclesiology, more so than our theology.

When I began this process, I knew our testimonies would be different from the free-church tradition of Spirit-filled praise. Many churchgoers, when asked to speak about what we believe, speak instead about what we have experienced. While some churches are concerned with points of doctrine, what came out in our testimonies were stories about church. We reflected less on Jesus in a personal way, and more on the community gathered in his name—but I believe that Christ is in the midst of it all.

Church members reflect to one another how God has called us to be a church, telling one another when they think the vision has gone astray, rejoicing in hope when it seems to be the right vision. Testimonies often took us back to our vision, reminding us when we had strayed from it. Jonathan's testimony reminded us of our congregation's vision, along with a small correction for us about locking our doors. We heard these words from a "PK," a preacher's kid:

Jonathan

You would think it easy for this PK to find a church home to worship God. Not so. My search for a church home took me all over New Haven, Branford, and Hamden—literally hundreds of times past the closed, white doors of Redeemer on many-a-Sunday morn. The closed doors made me feel like I wasn't welcome, like there was some secret way in. They seemed to signify the same closed-mindedness of most church communities I visited in and around New Haven. I think I'm going to have to talk with the deacons about this one.

I didn't see what made this community different until I joined a worship service at the invitation of your steward of music, who shall remain anonymous but whose initials are M.B. I was drawn first by who sat in the pews and the diversity of races and ages. The music was moving and inspiring, and offered with genuine love and passion. The word was spoken with provocative insight and inspired brilliance. So what finally tipped the scales for this PK to make a home at Redeemer? Something similar to the palms that welcomed Christ into Jerusalem—and that welcoming reads as follows:

We are the Church of the Redeemer, United Church of Christ, an inclusive community committed to the worship of God, the work of justice, and the recognition of our common humanity in the struggles of life.

We follow Jesus Christ, who welcomes all people to his table. We celebrate the rich diversity of God's people: in race, gender, age, sexual orientation, physical and mental abilities, marital and economic status and culture.

Join us on a journey of the Holy Spirit, where faith and intellect meet, learning never ends, and music and the arts draw us closer to our Creator.

Thanks for opening those doors.

In those words, Jonathan not only reminded us of our vision, as expressed through a statement we had crafted and voted on as a congregation, but in reading our vision statement out loud to the church, he allowed us to hear it with fresh ears and reminded us to unlock those church doors as well. While every testimony was not that explicit in the vision it cast, they all cast one. The aspects of church life people chose to highlight, from a warm welcome to a provocative discussion of a social issue, all said something to us about what the testifier believed the church should be. Sometimes these words challenged or surprised us into a better way of being the church. It was intriguing to hear people's many visions of what we should be in the diversity of Christ's body.

Testimony Is Risky

But what if someone were to stand up and offer a cruel or crazy vision? What if someone were to use the moment to bring forth a grudge or an agenda that reflected poorly on the church? Testimony is a risky practice, but if it is a regular one, you can rest assured that the following Sunday someone could cast the vision again. It takes a confident church to introduce testimony, I suspect, one that is willing to face the unpredictable and to release some control. But it is in the very release of control that the blessings come.

I never wanted to read people's testimony beforehand, for it would have taken away the elements of surprise and expectation that fill the moment. I wanted to hear the testimonies as others heard them, immediate and fresh. Certainly, we will not always be pleasantly surprised by what is said, or how it is said, but the very idea of being open has value in and of itself. Churches can so easily become places where control and order shut out spontaneity. Worship that seeks to be comforting in its ritual can become boring, especially when the only creative voice comes from the pastoral staff week after week. Testimony opened worship up and I, as the pastor, used to being in control of so much of the service, longed to be surprised myself. So even when people offered to show me their testimonies or asked for editing, I avoided doing it. For people who are not used to speaking about their faith, the practice is risky enough without adding a layer of censorship to the process.

Testimony Is a Gift Given Freely

Just as hearing testimony is and needs to be risky, giving testimony can be risky too. We open ourselves up to be known by our community of faith in deeper ways than we used to know one another. What if someone does not care for your words? What if they end up feeling distant from you, rather than closer? Not everyone will want to take this risk, nor should everybody be expected to. I would resist a practice in which people are forced to give testimony, for instance as a requirement for joining the church, or a requirement to serve in leadership. Testimony should be offered as a gift.

Testimony is a gift freely given, albeit with an occasional bit of begging or prodding. People seem to understand that even when the words of a testimony do not connect to them, they have still been given a precious gift to be handled with care. Nobody should be forced into it or coerced. It is not a practice everyone should have to take the lead in. Besides, the listener plays as important a role as the speaker.

Testimony Creates Community and Revitalizes Worship

Over and over again, people told me that testimony was opening up our church, not only creating excitement in worship, but in the coffee hour discussions as well. We were making new friends, hearing new stories of faith, being woken up by the Word. Having offered testimonies three times in the previous four years, David commented: "I think the practice of testimony has been an important part of the revitalization of our congregation." Many church members echoed this theme. Newcomers often commented on what they learned about the church through listening to testimonies, from stories from our histories to ideas about where the church was headed. It added an element of anticipation to worship and helped us to grow deeper in our relationships with one another. David continued:

> For each of us who have participated, the reflection and clarification has been a transforming experience in itself. For the worship service, it creates an atmosphere of openness and trust, and a sense of personal connection. It also reflects the diversity of our congregation: although we are inspired by those who have gone before, there is no pattern to the nature of testimony, no sense that there is an expectation of a right way to do it, just a recognition that each story is part of the fabric.

That recognition, "that each story is part of the fabric" of the larger story of faith, is what pastors are forever trying to put across in their preaching. We hope that when we tell the old Bible stories, we are calling people into the larger story of God. In an individualistic culture, preachers run uphill trying to remind people that we are part of a larger salvation history that is much larger than any one individual experience. Testimony showed us that all the time. In the variety of testimonies, we began to see the connections among them. We saw that while a person might be talking about her grandfather's love of the Bible, and another person might be talking about ugly ties, in the end they were all pointing to the one true God. If all these stories in their variety could be connected to one church and one God, surely we were all connected to the God of history and to one another.

I wonder if people make these connections more easily when they hear from another layperson, one whom they cannot presume to be some sort of "super Christian." People expect the pastor to speak of faith and a connection to larger story. They get used to the pastor's ways of speaking and familiar ideas. But when a different layperson speaks week after week, they hear the same story told in so many ways, and can imagine where their own story might fit in God's history.

David's testimony alluded to that in his point about the diversity of experiences. By listening only to the pastor's experience of God, subjective and unique to the pastor, congregations get one perspective. But by listening to testimony, they hear a wide variety of ways God interacts with human beings, and there, in that mix, they may find themselves and look at their own life differently.

When we are exposed to a variety of faith stories, we may more readily accept the wideness of God's mercy, or as David put it, in hearing, we realize that there is no one "right way to do it, just a recognition that each story is part of the fabric." Listening to testimony helps us to find our thread in God's fabric, and to know that we are never alone in our journeys. We are called to live as disciples, calling one another into the walk with Christ in the world, and testimonies called us into new ways of living.

Testimony Strengthens Leadership and Evokes a Sense of Call

Many of those who spoke in church were already leaders in the congregation, but it seemed that after giving testimony, people stepped up their leadership. Sometimes they volunteered for a new ministry, or showed new enthusiasm for a project within the church. They became more likely to speak up at meetings and to offer their voice on issues facing the congregation. By making themselves known through their testimonies, they found they suddenly had more relationships in the congregation than they had had before speaking. Leaders who were already relational became more so, and people with few relationships built more. As people grew in their relationships with one another and to the church, we saw more people trying new things in leadership, rather than the same people doing the same jobs over and over again. We also saw people beginning to wonder if they were called to serve the church as pastors.

For a church of 225 members, we suddenly had a large number of people considering ordained ministry. After a few years of practicing testimony, we had four people in seminary, with four more seriously considering it. Our church was nationally recognized by the Fund for Theological Education for being a church that nurtures so many people into the ministry. While we are near a divinity school, most of these people were nurtured in their faith and call right there at Church of the Redeemer, and all of them had given testimonies as part of their journey.

I believe that in giving testimony, a number of people were awakened to a call to preach. The stretch of standing up bravely and speaking in front of the church made them consider doing so on a more regular basis. As people hear the calls come through in one another's testimonies, I believe they also start to examine their own calls more seriously. One crisis the church faces today is whether or not gifted people will hear God's call to the ministry, so that future generations will have the leaders they need. Testimony opened a number of people's ears to a call that, without testimony, might not have emerged.

Testimony Is Transformational

I began to notice recently that testimonies are usually stories about some sort of transformation. They often tell a story that could be summed up: "I used to feel, or be, or behave this way, but now something has changed." So often, people reflected on a new way of being that had opened up to them through their participation in the church community. They might point out a lesson learned or a behavior changed, as Alan did one Sunday, when he described how his faith had shaped his business travel habits after the September 11, 2001, terrorist attack on the World Trade Center.

Alan

Speaking of journeys, many of you know that I fly to central Louisiana each month to work. Traveling is not much fun any longer. My trip is much longer, much more arduous, and humorless. Security people, National Guardsmen, police-women, flight attendants, and bomb-dog handlers are all very serious about their work. Travelers face personally intrusive inspections, including hands-on body searches. These are simply signs of the times. There is so much uncertainty in our lives these days: the downturn in the economy and its effects on each of us; the war and concerns about all those who are suffering as a result of our nation's fight against terrorism; and struggles closer to home here in New Haven.

In the face of all of this, you might ask me if I changed, and I would have to admit that I have. In recent months, I had begun to use my DVD player with my noise-blanking headset to isolate myself during the five-and-a-half hours that I am in the air. This is just not typical of me, since I believe that my Christian journey is embodied in my desire to be open and kind to all of God's people, including strangers. Let me tell you that nothing makes me happier than extending a hand of greeting to visitors here on Sunday mornings. I had always made it a point to meet the person sitting next to me on flights and to be kind and appreciative of the folks I meet along the way.

After 9/11, I must admit that I have retreated into myself while flying. Perhaps responding to everyone else's dour attitudes, I had begun to purposefully separate myself from others on the journey. Is this a positive Christian attitude? The answer is no.

Recently I've been wondering what I might do to deepen my faith, and I believe that being open to God's messages every day is one way to do that. I came to this realization as a result of a recent experience on one of my trips.

Alan went on to tell a wonderful story about how, after watching his DVD the whole trip, he finally spoke to his neighbor on the plane as they landed, only to discover the man was an astronaut. As the man continued his story, Alan said he wished he had met him earlier.

Knowing that I had spent several hours next to a most interesting person but only enjoyed 10 minutes of conversation with him made me realize that in my new isolation, I could be missing many opportunities to know God on this journey of life. Each of us will be on this journey through Lent, and my prayer for all of us is that we be open to the opportunities to know God and to see his work in the world.

For all of us, Lent is a time of renewal and promise. For me, it means I'm back on the road again with the grace of God! I say a prayer and I reach out to befriend everyone I come in contact with.

This was a story of transformation, as so many of the stories were. This story gave the rest of us an idea about how we might make our faith a way of life and how to get back on track when we were temporarily derailed from that way of life. Alan ended with a call to all of us to be transformed and to look out for the stranger, not just here at church but wherever our lives took us.

Testimonies transformed our church. We were opened up to the strangers among us in new ways and taught that the life of faith is always a journey of transformation. People seemed to become more honest in their stories about hardship and struggle. We became more open to changing our minds, since so many testimonies spoke of doing just that. Rather than resist it, we came to expect transformation, even look forward to it.

Testimony Happens in a Particular Moment in Time

One Sunday, we heard from Kassie who, unlike so many others, chose to stand up in front of the congregation without a note in her hand. She offered a testimony that was spontaneous, the story of her conversion decades ago, the moment

when, as she stood in her kitchen listening to an audio re-
cording of a well-known preacher, she accepted Jesus as her
savior. She then went on to talk about what it had felt for her
to be in the wilderness, believing in God's promises but struggling with the challenges of life as well, long after her conversion experience.

Perhaps the most interesting note was that she had not
known what she would say until the day before, when she
had shown up for the church cleanup day. When washing down
the pews, the testimony words had started to come to her.
That small labor of hospitality opened her up to what she was
to say the next day. As she scrubbed the pews, her mind was
freed up to imagine what word God had for her the next day.

The fact that I can't reconstruct Kassie's testimony word
for word reminds me that testimony is a practice for which
you have to be present—even when the person speaks from
notes. The inflections of the voice, the choked word, the self-
conscious laugh—all these shape the testimony as much as the
words that were prepared. Reading words on paper is so different from hearing them spoken in a whisper of emotion, or
bellowed out with great humor, or stumbled over in nervousness. A hand that delicately brushes hair out of the speaker's
face, or a dropped note card, or even the speaker's outfit—all
add to the complexity of the moment. None of this can be
bottled up or captured after the moment itself; we can merely
recall and reconstruct. With testimony, you've got to be there.

Testimony is also shaped by the people who listen and
attend to what is being said in that moment. Their reactions,
their hearts, will never arrive on paper. We cannot possibly
know all the reactions taking place, the gasps, or even the
yawns that all are part of the event.

Also present are the saints who have gone before us, a
cloud of witnesses we will recognize another day. I do not

think you can separate a moment of testimony from all the generations who have passed away but whose words came before and shaped the community, its practices, and its ways, and somehow brought us to this point. All of them are gathered in a particular moment of time.

In the end, we do not have the ability to freeze a moment of testimony in time. Whenever we retell a story, we change it in some way. Even the words of the testimonies in this book cannot replicate the moment in which they were given. And finally Kassie's story, with no script left behind, remains recorded only on the hearts that heard it that day, and of course in God's heart as well.

Growing in the Practices of Faith

In *After Virtue*, philosopher Alasdair MacIntyre tells us that throwing a football pass is not a practice, but that the game of football is. "Every practice requires a certain kind of relationship between those who participate in it."[1] Testimony depends upon relationship as well. The testifier needs others to listen, a community shaped over time by shared practices. Testimony goes so much deeper than one individual's deep thoughts. Other players (other members of the faith community) are involved in a game whose rules (Christian practices) we players cannot simply make up as we go along and yet whose rules may change as the playing community sees fit, as our practices change or develop over time. Christian practices exist in community and over time. And of course, another player, namely God, is involved. So Christian practices point us beyond ourselves—as the practice of testimony did.

Practices are usually not performed in isolation from one another; one practice points and leads to another. In this book, I have linked the testimonies by the practices they point to.

But I also could have written a book about various practices and the testimonies they later inspired. Practices can feed one another in an endless loop. For example, an experience of hospitality might lead to a testimony about hospitality that in turn inspires another person in the practice of hospitality. But in a society that privileges individual growth over the practices of a community sustained over time, we need a community to encourage and foster that feedback loop, lest we forget that we are indeed practicing as part of something larger than ourselves.

Already a believer in these practices, I as a minister still have an endless capacity for amnesia. We heard many of these testimonies during the weeks leading up to Easter. Lent is that mysterious season when ministers whip themselves into a frenzy of activity, telling everyone else to calm down and reflect. Typically for the season, I preached quiet closeness with God and practiced frantic activity. Lent is the season most likely to reveal my hypocrisy of hardly practicing what I preached. But I know I yearned to.

Gracefully, it's not just our own practices that keep us close to God. Sometimes, when we're drifting, someone else's practice may be the rope that pulls us back in. In the middle of one particularly stressful Lent, how I needed to hear the Lenten testimonies of others to be reminded of their truth once again. How I needed their words to see that even as I could not practice with the grace of those who offered their words, their practice embraced me too.

So many other times, testimonies strengthened me in my work as a pastor. In the busiest seasons of a minister's year, in those times when my own preaching felt dry, I was reminded in the testimonies I heard that it was not all up to me. God's grace broke in through the words of us ordinary people all the time. We came to know one another and God with a sharpness I could never have imagined in community. Often I was called back once again to the beautiful vision of the church that had made me want to serve it full time.

Over and over, a generous God shined through in words about dolls, ties, committees, old churches, and new ones. A practice that at first seemed borrowed from other traditions or plucked artificially from a history long passed now belonged to us at Church of the Redeemer. Our words made the practice of testimony our own, and now it owns us, as surely as it has owned those throughout the centuries who have boldly stood in front of one another and haltingly spoken of things too mysterious to be taken lightly.

When I think of all I have received in the practice of testimony at Church of the Redeemer, I sense these small constellations of words around me, conjuring up a more beautiful starlit sky within which sits a cloud of witnesses who say things like this:

> Each story is part of the fabric.
> You must practice your faith, not try to fit it in around
>   other things in your schedule.
> I felt that I had found home.
> I say a prayer and I reach out to befriend everyone I
>   come in contact with.
> Holy Smoke! What a change!
> My experiences of the worship and community here
>   have affected a very significant conversion within my
>   heart and mind.
> I felt radiant, lighter than air.
> You make this church unique.
> Thanks for opening those doors.

So that's my testimony.

NOTES

Preface
1. Ann Wilcox, Stockbridge "Experiences," c. 1830-1833, First Congregational Church Records, HC1972.005.6, Stockbridge Library Association Historical Collection. My thanks to Kenneth P. Minkema of Yale University for identifying this source.

Introduction, Tell It Like It Is
1. Thomas Hoyt, "Testimony," in *Practicing Our Faith: A Way of Life for a Searching People,* ed. Dorothy C. Bass (San Francisco: Jossey-Bass Publishers, 1997), 93–94.
2. C. Kirk Hadaway and David R. Roozen, *Rerouting the Protestant Mainstream* (Nashville: Abigndon Press, 1995), 65.
3. Alasdair MacIntyre, *After Virtue: A Study in Moral Theory* (Notre Dame, Ind.: University of Notre Dame Press, 1997), 190.

Chapter 1, The Household of the Heart
1. Christine Pohl, *Making Room: Recovering Hospitality as a Christian Tradition* (Grand Rapids: Eerdmans, 1999), 41–42.
2. Ibid., 42.

Chapter 2, To Join or Not to Join?
1. Nancy T. Ammerman, "Culture and Identity in the Congregation," in eds, Nancy T. Ammerman, Jackson W. Carroll, Carl

S. Dudley, and William McKinney, *Studying Congregations: A New Handbook* (Nashville: Abingdon Press, 1998), 89.

Chapter 3, Money: We Need to Talk About It
1. Sharon Daloz Parks, "Household Economics," in *Practicing Our Faith*, 45.
2. Robert Wuthnow, *Poor Richard's Principle* (Princeton, N.J.: Princeton University Press, 1996), 294.
3. Ibid., 299.
4. Ibid., 63. Unfortunately, as a diverse and interracial church, we went on to discover that Taylor, for all his new ideas, had been a slave owner and on the wrong side of the key issue of his day. So his New England largeness of liberality turned out to have been rather thin indeed. But as our congregation's historical spiritual ancestor, his words still give me food for thought even as I understand his character to have been flawed.
5. Ibid.

Chapter 4, The Gift of Time
1. Dorothy C. Bass, "Keeping Sabbath," in *Practicing Our Faith*, 76.

Chapter 9, Speaking of Grief
1. Amy Plantinga Pauw, "Dying Well," in *Practicing Our Faith*, 163–164.

Chapter 10, Building Stronger Leaders
1. Eugene Peterson, "On Being Unnecessary," in *Pastor*, ed. William H. Willimon (Nashville: Abingdon Press, 2002), 91–93.

Chapter 13, Speak the Vision
1. MacIntyre, 191.

BIBLIOGRAPHY

Ammerman, Nancy Tatom. *Congregation and Community.* Nashville: Abingdon Press, 1997.

Ammerman, Nancy T., Jackson Carroll, Carl S. Dudley, and Will McKinney, eds. *Studying Congregations: A New Handbook.* Nashville: Abingdon Press, 1998.

Arbuckle, Gerald R. *Earthing the Gospel: An Inculcation Handbook for the Pastoral Worker.* Maryknoll, N.Y.: Orbis, 1990.

Bass, Dorothy C., ed. *Practicing Our Faith: A Way of Life for a Searching People.* San Francisco: Jossey-Bass Publishers, 1997.

Chaves, Mark, and Sharon L. Miller, eds. *Financing American Religion.* Walnut Creek, Calif.: Alta Mira Press, 1999.

Dudley, Carl, Jackson Carroll, and James P. Wind, eds. *Carriers of Faith: Lessons from Congregational Studies.* Louisville: Westminster John Knox Press, 1989.

Dykstra, Craig. *Growing in the Practices of the Faith: Education and Christian Practices.* Louisville: Geneva Press, 1999.

Hadaway, C. Kirk, and David R. Roozen. *Rerouting the Protestant Mainstream: Sources of Growth and Opportunities for Change.* Nashville: Abingdon Press, 1995.

Hoge, Dean, Patrick McNamara, and Charles Zech, eds. *Plain Talk About Churches and Money.* Herndon, Va.: Alban Institute, 1998.

Hudnut-Beumler, James. *Generous Saints: Congregations Rethinking Ethics and Money.* Bethesda, Md.: Alban Institute, 1999.

MacIntyre, Alasdair. *After Virtue: A Study in Moral Theory.* Notre Dame, Ind.: University of Notre Dame Press, 1997.

Mudge, Lewis, and James Poling. *Formation and Reflection: The Promise of Practical Theology,* Philadelphia: Fortress Press, 1987.

Straw, Joseph. "Is It Time the Suburbs Did More to Share the Wealth?" *New Haven Register,* February 17, 2002, sec. A.

Wheeler, Sondra Ely. *Wealth as Peril and Obligation: The New Testament on Possessions.* Grand Rapids: Eerdmans, 1995.

Whitehead, James D., and Evelyn Eaton Whitehead. *Method in Ministry: Theological Reflection and Christian Ministry.* New York: The Seabury Press, 1983.

Wilcox, Ann. Stockbridge. "Experiences," c. 1830–1833, Stockbridge Library Association, Historical Collection.

Willhauk, Susan, and Jacqulyn Thorpe. *The Web of Women's Leadership: Recasting Congregational Ministry.* Nashville: Abingdon Press, 2001.

Willimon, William H., ed. *Pastor: A Reader for Ordained Ministry.* Nashville: Abingdon Press, 2002.

Wuthnow, Robert. *Poor Richard's Principle: Recovering the American Dream through the Moral Dimension of Work, Business, and Money.* Princeton: Princeton University Press, 1996.

Zikmund, Barbara Brown, Adair T. Lummis, and Patricia Mei Chang. *Clergy Women: An Uphill Calling.* Louisville: Westminster John Knox Press, 1998.